The Complexities of Water

Biological Regionalism:
Bagmati River,
Kathmandu Valley, Nepal

Alberto Rey
Jason Dilworth

This marigold chain was strung around a shrine between Pashupatinath and Gueshwori Temples in Kathmandu. Marigolds symbolize trust in the Gods and their power to overcome obstacles and evils. The strong odor also keeps flies from the offerings.

The Complexities of Water
Biological Regionalism:
Bagmati River,
Kathmandu Valley, Nepal

Alberto Rey
Jason Dilworth

www.BagmatiRiverArtProject.com

Published by:

 Canadaway Press
Fredonia, New York 14063

© 2016 Alberto Rey
Charts and figures taken from the Bagmati River Expedition 2015.
Nepal River Conservation Trust & Biosphere Association.

Translation from English to Nepali by Prashant Das

Project made possible with the support of the Kathmandu Contemporary Art Centre, Kathmandu, Nepal

Text and Images unless otherwise noted: Alberto Rey
Design: Jason Dilworth

Printed in China

onthemark.net
75-5660 Kopiko St #C7 – 105
Kailua-Kona, HI 96740

ISBN: 978-0-9979644-0-0

Dedicated to the Nepali People

नेपाली जनताप्रति समर्पित

Contents

The Bagmati River Art Project could not have happened without the support of a great deal of individuals who envisioned the value of the project when it was nothing more than an optimistic idea for social and environmental change. The Project has grown to include this publication, a documentary video, an interactive website, and public health brochures and posters all of which will be included in an exhibition at the Siddhartha Gallery in Kathmandu, Nepal. The entire project will then tour the United States through the support, organization and guidance of the Burchfield Penney Art Center in Buffalo.

Jason Dilworth and Alberto Rey would like to thank the following individuals and organizations for their support:

United States:
Erin Cooper
Zachary Schneider
Matthew Dorn
Patrick Courts
William Mariani
Felicia Meila
Janis C Johnson
Douglas Manly
Charles Lanzieri
Andrew Dorn
Mirta Rice
Wyatt Arthurs
Jeff Dorn
Dan R Talley
Bill and Jill Jedlicka
Rob Benigno
Patricia Briggs
Elizabeth C Johnson
Phillip K Jensen
Brian Schuliger
Matt Benson
Michael Conley
Kalil Boghdan
Ann Burns
Sandy Smith Cunningham
Rosie Sanden
David Munschauer
Casey Falco
Horst and Elizabeth Weber

Lisa Beyer Scanlon
Serina Beauparlant
Richard Alexander
Rosemary Lombardo
Patricia Saville
James Hurtgen
Joel P. Johnson
Rebecca White
Mary Myers
William & Holly Cumberland
Christopher Keffer
Lynette M. Bosch
Jeffrey T. Innes
Edward Weidenbach
Jorge Almeida
Brett McConnell
Jenna Edwards
David Benson
Jenifer Veazey
J Diane Martonis
Suzanne Clements
Chris Bishop
Rosemary Lombardo
Stephen Martonis
David Johnson
Scott Propeack
Anthony Bannon
Heather Gring
Janeil Rey
David Gillette

Ralph Blasting
Robert Booth
Mike Jabot
Rhonda Byrne
Judith M Horowitz
Virginia Horvath
Terry Brown
Heidi M Moldenhauer
Paul Benson
Nick Gunner
Jorge Gracia
Christine Doolittle
Shannon Dorsey
Tom and Mary Gordon
Mike Rechlin
Sam Mix
Blair Volpe
Pujan Gandharba
Amrit Gandhari
Alex Maiola
Nepal:
Sangeeta Thapa
Sujan Chitrakar
Sunil Shrestha
Sharad (Anil) Parajuli
Pujan Gandharba
Amrit Gandhari
Deep Narayan Shah
Ram Devi Tachamo Shah
Shristi Vaidya

NayanTara Kakshapati
Shikhar Bhattarai
Bibhuti Jha
Bandana Pradhan
Leela Mani Poudel
Ujala Shrestha
Billy Forbes
Himalaya Shumsher J.B. Rana
Isabelle Onians
Abhaya Joshi
Smriti Basnet
Sujan G Amatya
Erina Tamrakar
Asha Dangol
Swodesh Shakya
Saajan Shakya
John L. Carwile
Rajendra Suwal
Shikha Khetan
Jeff Davids
Smriti Basnet
Carol Milner
William Holton
David Fedak
Fred & Judy Gregory
Stephanie Lewthwaite
Bidhuti Ranjan Jha
Asha Dangol
Erina Tamrakar
Suresh Man Lakhe

Outside of Golden Temple in Patan, one can find temples with floral offerings. floral offerings.

St. John's

4 hours into flight from philly to Boston - just
past Cape Farwel, Greenland coming up to Iceland

March 12, 2016   2:16 pm

March 12, 2016 - Qatar Airways - QR 728 - Seat 25A - two 3 hours and twenty minutes into flight and 8 hours and 53 minutes left - Flying below southern tip of Cape Farrel, Greenland - 1:25 pm - 2:10 pm

Too dARK

Drawing of the airplane's interior from Alberto's seat on the way to Doha, Qatar.

Project background

While doing research in Kathmandu, I was often asked why an artist from the United States would start a project documenting a polluted river in a small country on the other side of the globe. After giving the question some thought, I looked back at my life and questioned how I had arrived at this point. I realized that some childhood experiences shaped the way my career evolved. For me it started in the late 1960s to early 70s, which is coincidentally around the same time that the Bagmati River's pollution picked up speed. After receiving political asylum from Cuba, my family settled in a small, rural, coal-mining town in western Pennsylvania where my father taught Spanish at the local high school and my mother worked as a seamstress at a factory. At the end of every school year, we would drive down to Miami and spend our entire summer with our extended family. It is here where my cousin, Omar, and I would escape the hottest months of southern Florida by snorkeling for countless hours in the same Gulf Stream that flowed past Havana, Cuba where I was born. Although Miami was developing quickly during this time, we found respite in the quiet image-rich underwater world that was located a few feet from shore. It was these experiences that began my curiosity about everything related to water. Upon my return back north, I would spend the cold winters constantly drawing everything around me, dreaming about floating on warm tropical currents and reading about the lifecycles of dolphins, sharks and tropical fish.

अनुसन्धानको क्रममा मलाई प्राय किन आधी संसार पारीबाट एक अमेरिकी कलाकार एउटा सानो देशमा प्रदूषित नदीको अभिलेखिकरण गर्न इच्छुक भयो भन्ने प्रश्न सोधिने गरिएको थियो । धेरै पटक यो प्रश्न सोधिएपछि मलाई पछाडी फर्केर आफ्नो जीवन न्यालेर हेर्न मन लाग्यो । मेरो बाल्यक(ालका केही अनुभवहरुले मेरो व्यावसायीक जीवनलाई आकार दिएको हुनुपर्दछ भन्ने मलाई आभाष भयो । संयोगवश यसको सुरुआत त्यसै बेला भएको थियो जब बागमती नदीमा प्रदूषणले गती लिंदै थियो, अर्थात सन १९६० को अन्त्यदेखि १९७० को सुरुआततिर । अमेरीकामा राजनैतिक शरण पाएपछि हाम्रो परिवार क्युवाबाट पश्चिमि पेन्सिलभिनियामा कोइला खानी भएको एउटा सानो शहरमा बसाइ सर्यो। यहाँ मेरा पिताले स्थानिय उच्च विद्यालयमा स्प्यानिश भाषा पढाउनुहुन्थ्यो भने मेरी आमाले लुगा सिउने काम गर्नुहुन्थ्यो । हरेक शैक्षिक सत्रको अन्त्यमा हामी मायामी गएर आफ्नो संयुक्त परिवारका सदस्यहरुसँग ग्रीष्म ऋतु बिताउने गर्थ्यौं । यही त्यो ठाउँ थियो जहाँ म मेरो मामाको छोरा ओमारसँग दक्षिणी फ्लोरिडाको गर्मी छल्न मेरो जन्मस्थल क्युबाको हवाना शहर हुँदै बग्ने नहरमा पौडी खेल्दै समय बिताउँथे । मायामी शहर ठूलो परिवर्तनबाट गुज्रिरहँदा हामी पानीमुनीको शान्त संसारमा रमाइरहेका थियौं । बाल्यकालको यही अनुभवले मभित्र पानीमुनीको संसारप्रति जिज्ञासा जगायो । मायामीबाट फर्केपछि म जाडो महिना आफ्नो वरिपरिका सबै वस्तुहरुको चित्र कोर्दै र न्यानो पानीको सतहमाथि बग्दै गरेको कल्पनामा र डलफिन, शार्क तथा अन्य उष्ण प्रदेशिय माछाको जीवनी बारे सोच्दै बिताउँथे ।

By the time I went to college, I was convinced that I would become a marine biologist but, under the guidance of one of my art professors, I decided to continue with my artistic studies instead. I did not realize that decades later I would be able to combine both fields.

In the 1990's, while teaching drawing and painting at a small college in western New York, I was introduced to fly-fishing and my love for science was rekindled. As I began studying lifecycles of regional fish and the insects that they fed on, I also became intrigued with the connections between the chemistry of the water where they lived and the history of the settlements where streams flowed. It was during this time that I became interested in how science and art worked together in American and European history in the 1800's. The Hudson River School artists in the United States had documented the spirituality of their new nation's botany, biology and geology through paintings. While in Europe, Alexander von Humboldt and his contemporaries were publishing very popular illustrated scientific volumes about their travels around the world.

I began my own travels around the western hemisphere as I fly-fished and documented the landscapes and fish species through drawings, photographs, paintings and videos. On certain occasions I was presented with opportunities through residencies to expand my research on specific regions. I carefully investigated the relationship between water, urban migration, aquatic biology, economics, pollution and art. These investigations were then presented through multimedia installations in galleries and museums. These installations created accessible connections between complicated issues. These series of investigations and installations were titled The Biological Regionalism Series.

An installation shot of Biological Regionalism: Scajaquada Creek, Erie County, New York, USA at the Burchfield Penney Art Center, Buffalo, NY.

Been Trap Canyon - below Ennis Lake - 8/7/01 - 6:35 pm

Been Trap Canyon - Upper Madison River - 8/07/01 -
had a great day earlier that day at Upper Canyon
Outfitters fishing the Ruby River - using a
club sandwiches and a royal wulff was the
most effective way to get theatrical rises
and 14"-16" rainbows & browns - I landed about
12-15 of them in 2½ hours and had many
misses

and   - royal wulff - I had to use
        tippet because the fish were such good

कलेज पुग्दासम्म म समुद्री जीववैज्ञानिक बन्नेमा विश्वस्त भइसकेको थिएँ तर एक जना कलाका प्राध्यापकको प्रेरणाले मैले मेरो कलाको अध्ययनलाई निरन्तरता दिने निर्णय गरेँ । त्यती खेर मैले सोचेको थिइन कि दशकौं पछि म यो दुवै क्षेत्रलाई जोड्ने काम गर्नेछु भनेर ।

सन् १९९० को दसकतिर पश्चिमी न्यू योर्करिथत एक कलेजमा चित्रकला पढाइरहँदा म फ्लाइ(फिशिङ (कृत्रिम झिँगाको महत्तले माछा मार्ने तरिका) सँग परिचित भएँ र विज्ञानप्रतिको मेरो मोह फेरी जागृत भयो । जब मैले स्थानिय माछा र तिनीहरुले खाने साना कीराहरुबारे पढ्न थालेँ, तिनीहरु बस्ने पानीको रसायन विज्ञान र ती खोलाहरु बग्ने स्थानहरुको इतिहासप्रति मेरो चासो बढ्दै गयो । त्यही बेला नै म सन् १८०० तिर अमेरिका र युरोपमा हुने गरेको कला र विज्ञानबिचको समन्वयप्रति आकर्षित भएँ । अमेरिकामा हड्सन रिभर स्कूलका कलाकारले त्यस राष्ट्रको वनस्पति विज्ञान, जीव विज्ञान तथा भूविज्ञानको आध्यात्मिकतालाई प्रलेखीकरण गरेका थिए भने त्यही समयमा युरोपमा अलेक्जेन्डर भोन हम्बोल्ट र उहाँका समकालिनहरुले तिनीहरुका विश्व भ्रमणबारे रोचक वैज्ञानिक पत्रिका प्रकाशित गर्दै थिए ।

म पनि पश्चिमी गोलार्द्धको यात्रामा निस्केँ र यात्राका क्रममा फ्लाइ फिशिङ गर्नुका साथै तस्वीर, चित्रकला तथा भिडियोमार्फत प्राकृतिक स्थलहरु र माछाका प्रजातीहरुको अभिलेखिकरन गर्ने काम पनि गर्न थालेँ । मैले रेसिडेन्सिहरुबाट केही खास क्षेत्रहरुको मेरो सोधलाई विस्तार गर्ने मौका पनि पाएँ । मैले ध्यानपूर्वक पानी, शहरी प्रवास, जलचर जीव विज्ञान, अर्थशास्त्र, प्रदुषण र कलाबिचको सम्बन्धमाथि खोज गरेँ । यी खोजहरुलाई ग्यालेरी तथा संग्रहालयमा मल्टिमिडिया इन्स्टलेशनहरुमार्फत मैले प्रदर्शीत गरेँ । 'द बायोलोजिकल रिजनलिजम सिरिज' शिर्षक भएका यी इन्स्टलेशनहरुले जटिल विषयहरुबिचको सरल संयोजन निर्माण गरे ।

It was during one of these museum installations in April of 2014 at the Burchfield Penney Art Center in Buffalo, New York that I was asked to consider starting a project about the Bagmati River that flowed through the middle of Kathmandu in Nepal. Before starting any investigation, I wanted to make sure that there was interest in this project from the community in the city. After some initial inquiries, it was clear that there was genuine support for the project, and I quickly received a residency at the Kathmandu Contemporary Art Center, and an exhibition at a well-respected contemporary art gallery, Siddhartha Art Gallery, was slated for the following year. The major earthquakes in April of 2015 delayed the exhibition date but provided an opportunity to extend the research and outreach. The two years of work on this project culminated in an exhibition, documentary, publication, website, and public health brochures and posters. The entire project was presented in Kathmandu in the fall of 2016 at the Siddhartha Art Gallery. The project then travelled to the Burchfield Penney Art Center where it began touring internationally.

न्यू योर्कको बफेलोस्थित बर्चफिल्ड आर्ट सेन्टरमा सन २०१४ को अप्रिल महीनामा यस्तै एक इन्स्टलेशन भइरहेको बेला कसैले मलाई काठमाडौँको मध्य भागबाट बग्ने बागमती नदीमाथि एक परियोजना गर्ने बारे सल्लाह दियो । तर यस परियोजनाको लागि सोध गर्नुभन्दा अगाडी मलाई यस परियोजनाप्रति स्थानिय समुदायमा कतिको चासो छ जान्न मन लाग्यो । सुरुआति सोधपूछ पछि यस परियोजनाप्रति समुदायमा यथेष्ट चासो रहेको थाहा पाएँ र चाँडै नै मैले काठमाडौँ कन्टेम्पररि आर्ट सेन्टरमा रेसिडेन्सीको मौका पाएँ र अर्को वर्षको लागि नै प्रतिष्ठित सिद्धार्थ आर्ट ग्यालेरीमा मेरो प्रदर्शनी हुने तय भयो । सन २०१५ को भूकम्पले प्रदर्शनीको मिति सरेपनि यसले परियोजनाको सोध र क्षेत्रलाई अझ फराकिलो बनाउन समय प्रदान गऱ्यो । यस परियोजनाका लागि गरिएको दुई वर्षको कार्यले अन्तत: प्रदर्शनी, वृत्तचित्र, प्रकाशन, वेभसाइट तथा जनस्वास्थ्य सम्बन्धी पोस्टर र पुस्तिकाको रुप लियो । सन २०१६ को शिशिर ऋतुतिर यसलाई सिद्धार्थ आर्ट ग्यालेरीमा प्रदर्शीत गरियो । त्यसपछि यो परियोजना बर्चफिल्ड पेन्नि आर्ट सेन्टर हुँदै अन्तर्राष्ट्रिय यात्रामा निस्कियो ।

Earthquake-damaged buildings throughout the Kathmandu Valley. Unfortunately, many thousand-year-old temples were flattened.

The Bagmati River Art Project tries to provide a diverse range of opportunities to access valuable information from the countless reports, plans and articles created over the past decade. This project was designed to inform individuals who continue to use the toxic river water for irrigation, bathing and other uses. It was also intended to empower communities to continue their constructive efforts and, in some circumstances, consider healthy alternatives that might improve the lives of their families and neighbors. We also hoped to provide a perspective to younger generations who do not remember a time when the Bagmati River was pure and a center of spiritual interaction.

The Bagmati River's degradation over the past four decades is not an uncommon tale and similar stories can be found in industrialized cities around the world. The uniqueness of the river is its religious and cultural importance to the country and culture. Our intention was for this project to tour other destinations with similar issues so that the plight of this river and the proactive role of Kathmandu Valley's community could encourage positive action in other locations around the world.

बागमती रिभर आर्ट प्रोजेक्ट (बागमती नदी कला परियोजना) ले विगतका दसकहरुमा संकलित थुप्रै प्रतिवेदन, योजना तथा लेखहरुबाट महत्वपूर्ण तथ्यहरु प्राप्त गर्ने विविध मौका प्रदान गर्छ । यो परियोजनाको उद्देश्य दिनहुँ सिचाईं, नुहाउन तथा अन्य कामका लागि बागमतीको विषाक्त पानी प्रयोग गर्ने व्यक्तिहरुलाई सूचित गर्ने रहेको थियो । यसका साथै यो परियोजनाको लक्ष्य समुदायलाई आफ्नो रचनात्मक प्रयासहरुलाई निरंतरता दिन र आफ्नो तथा आफ्नो परिवारको सुस्वास्थ्यका लागि स्वस्थकर विकल्प खोज्न सक्षम बनाउनु पनि थियो । हामीले नयाँ पुस्तालाई, जो बागमती नदी सफा र आध्यात्मिक क्रियाकलापको केन्द्र रहेको समयबारे अनभिज्ञ छन्, बागमती नदीप्रति नयाँ दृष्टिकोण प्रदान गर्ने आशा पनि राखेका थियौं ।

विगत चार दसकमा बागमती नदी प्रदुषित हुनु कुनै नौलो कुरा होइन र यस्ता उदाहरणहरु विश्वका अन्य अधोगिक शहरहरुमा प्रशस्त रुपमा पाउन सकिन्छन् । तर बागमती नदीप्रति समाजमा रहेको धार्मिक तथा सांस्कृतिक महत्वले यसलाई अरुभन्दा पृथक बनाउँछ । हामी यो परियोजना लिएर यस्तै समस्या रहेका अन्य स्थानमा गई बागमती नदीको व्यथा र काठमाडौं उपत्यकाको समुदायको सक्रियताबाट अन्य ठाउँमा पनि सकारात्मक परिवर्तन ल्याउन चाहन्थ्यौं ।

The Patan Museum provided this photograph of Pashupatinath by Dr. Kurt Boeck from 1900.

Nepal, and specifically Kathmandu Valley, even with all its challenges, remains a location that forever haunts those who visit it. In my research, I have talked to people who had visited the region once 50 years ago to others who continue to return annually. They all have fond memories of the generous nature of the residents, the exoticness of the region, the spirituality that emanates throughout the valley, and a lingering sadness for what it has become.

नेपाल, अझ काठमाडौँ उपत्यका, थुप्रै चुनौतिहरुबिच पनि यहाँ आउने मानिसहरुको मनमा छाप पार्न सक्षम भइरहन्छ । मैले आफ्नो खोजको क्रममा ५० वर्ष अगाडी यहाँ आएका र हरेक वर्ष आइराख्ने दुवै खालका मान्छेहरुसँग कुरा गरेँ । तिनीहरुको सम्झनामा अहिले पनि नेपालीहरुको उदारता, यस क्षेत्रको सुन्दरता र उपत्यकामा अनुभव हुने आध्यात्म तथा यसमा आएको दुःखद बदलावको झल्को आइरहन्छ ।

Here is another photograph of Pashupatinath from over half a century later. This image was provided by the Mukunda Bahadur Shrestha Collection from the Nepal Picture Library.

Due to lack of electricity during most of the evening, we walked back to our hotel at Shakya House guided by solar powered led lights in the shops.

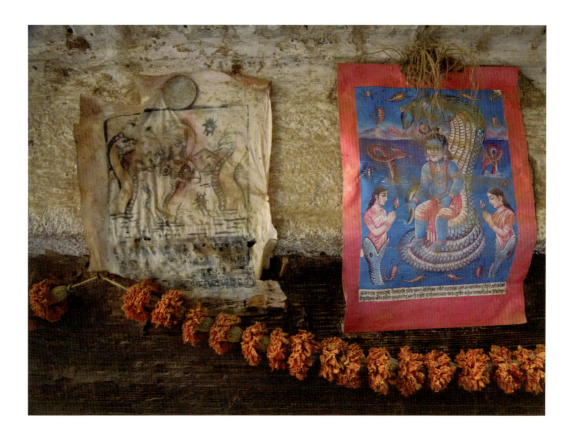

Nepalese residents secure pictures of Naag (the serpent god) pictures over their doorways with cow dung and offer foods to the god to protect the home from lightning, fire, snakes and scorpions.

Land of Contradictions

The Bagmati River, which flows through the center of Kathmandu Valley, is part of a complicated environmental and cultural narrative that is full of contradictions. The river flows through the center of a country that has more fresh water than most nations in the world, and yet, scarcity of water is one of its most urgent problems. Nepal is a poor country with high hydroelectric potential but the Kathmandu Valley is often without electricity for half the day. Kathmandu has a long history of cultural and spiritual significance centered around the Bagmati, and yet, the river has now become an open sewer, which flows through the center of the third most polluted city in the world. The river flows through a spiritually-important valley with seven UNESCO Heritage sites and over 350 important cultural locations. Many of these are slowly being sold off as private property, being converted to public buildings or being crowded out by developments. The valley has a plethora of environmental regulations, but the government does not enforce most of them. Kathmandu's main pollution issue is sewage disposal; however, it has five sewage treatment plants with only one working periodically. The population growth in the Valley continues to increase between 5 to 7 percent annually making it one of the fastest growing regions in South Asia, but there still remains virtually no urban planning. One would expect that the residents would be bitter from the chaotic nature of the city and the disfunctionality of the government but, instead, they are willing to help. They aspire to better their condition and are spiritually active everyday.

अन्तरविरोधहरुको भूमि

काठमाडौँको मध्यबाट बग्ने बागमती नदी अन्तरविरोधहरुले भरिपूर्ण यहाँको जटील पर्यावरण र सांस्कृतिक परिवेशको वर्णन गर्छ । यो नदी यस्तो देशको मध्यभागबाट बग्छ जहाँ अरु धेरै देशहरुको तुलनामा सबैभन्दा धेरै जलस्रोत छ तर पनि यसलाई पानीको अभावले पिरोलिरहेको हुन्छ । जलविद्युतको अथाह सम्भावना रहेको यस देशको राजधानीमा दिनको आधी समय बिजुली हुँदैन । वर्षौसम्म सांस्कृतिक र धार्मिक महत्वको केन्द्र रहेको बागमती अहिले विश्वको तेस्रो सर्वाधिक प्रदूषित शहरको ढलमा परिवर्तित भएको छ । आध्यात्मिक रुपले महत्वपूर्ण रहेको बागमती नदीको यस शहरगा युनेस्कोमा सूचित ७ वटा सम्पदाहरु र ३५० भन्दा बढी सांस्कृतिक रुपले महत्वपूर्ण स्थलहरु छन् । यीमध्ये धेरै जसो निजी सम्पति वा सार्वजनिक भवनमा परिवर्तित हुँदै छन् वा शहरी वीकासको भीडमा ओभ्रेल हुँदै छन् । नेपालमा पर्यावरण सम्बन्धी थुप्रै नियमहरु भएपनि सरकारले कुनैपनि नियम लागू गर्न सकेको छैन । काठमाडौँको प्रदुषणको मुख्य समस्या ढल निकास रहेका छ । यहाँ रहेका ५ वटा ढल निकास प्रणालीमध्ये मात्र एक वटा सञ्चालनमा छ ।

In Kathmandu's Durbur Square there is a large wall relief of the Hindu god Shiva as Bhairav, goddess of destruction.

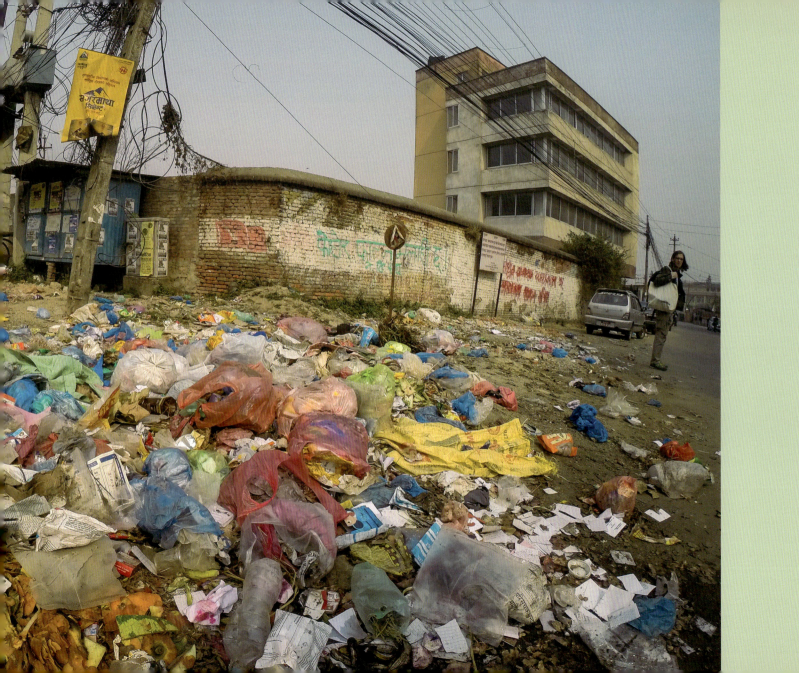

These contradictions create a compelling yet frustrating story that is, unfortunately, common. Around 90 percent of developing countries continue to dispose of all their untreated wastewater directly into nearby bodies of water, and globally, two million tons of human waste are released daily. As a consequence, half of the hospital beds in the world, as is the case in Kathmandu, are being used by patients suffering from water-borne illnesses that will kill more people than any form of violence including wars. These effects can be even more concentrated in cities where half of the world's population now lives and where 80 percent of all carbon dioxide (CO_2) is emitted. In the United States, pollution has affected 40% of the rivers and 46% of the lakes, which are now considered unhealthy to fish, dangerous to swim and inhospitable to the survival of aquatic life. Asia, which Nepal is part of, has the highest number of polluted rivers with three times the bacteria count from human waste than the global average. This worldwide problem is also affecting aquatic species, which have a five times higher extinction rate than that of terrestrial animals.

उपत्यकाको जनसंख्या वार्षिक ५७ प्रतिशतको दरले बढ्दै छ जसले यसलाई दक्षिण एसिया क्षेत्रकै सबैभन्दा तीव्र गतीमा बढ्दै गरेको क्षेत्र बनाउँछ तर यहाँ शहरी विकासको पर्याप्त योजना देखिदैन । शहरको अव्यवस्था र सरकारको असक्रियताले यहाँका बासिन्दाका मनमा तीतोपना ल्याउने अनुमान गर्न सकिन्छ तर तिनीहरु स्थितीमा सुधार आउने कुरामा आशावादी छन् र यसका लागि मद्दत गर्न तत्पर पनि ।

It is normal practice to dump garbage on the street with the hope that the city will take care of it. At times, the garbage is set on fire if it sits too long. This scene was outside of Yalamaya in Patan.

Communities around the world, like in the Kathmandu Valley, have started partnerships with nongovernment organizations (NGO's) to provide awareness to local communities of healthy practices that can improve neighborhoods and motivate government agencies to become more proactive. While this bottom-up approach is important in stemming practices contributing to the disposal of household waste in rivers and lakes, which creates health hazards, governments need to provide the infrastructure to address the bigger issues of sewage and water treatment, urban planning, garbage disposal and enforcement of environmental regulations.

यी अन्तरविरोधहरूले शसक्त तर निराशावादी चित्र प्रस्तुत गर्छन् जो दुर्भाग्यवश सामान्य पनि हो । १० प्रतिशत जति विकासशिल देशहरूमा प्रदुषित पानी नजिकै रहेको जल स्रोतमा निकास गर्ने गरिन्छ र संसारभरि दैनिक २० लाख टन मानव अपशिष्ट वा मल निस्कास्न हुन्छ । फलस्वरूप काठमाडौँका साथे संसारभरिका अस्पतालमा आधीभन्दा धेरै प्रदुषित पानीका बिरामीहरू छन् जसबाट हुने मृत्यु युद्ध र अन्य कुनै हिंसाबाट हुने मृत्युभन्दा बढी हुनेछ । अहिले संसारको आधि जनसंख्या शहरमा बसोबार गर्छ जहाँ ८० प्रतिशत कार्बन डाइअक्साइड उत्पादन हुन्छ । यस्ता शहरमा प्रदुषित पानीबाट हुने समस्या अझ गंभीर हुनसक्छ । संयुक्त राज्यमा प्रदुषणले गर्दा ४०% नदी र ४६% तालहरूलाई माछा मार्न, पौडी खेल्न र जल जीवनका लागि अयोग्य ठहर गरिएको छ । एसियामा, जहाँ नेपाल अवस्थित छ, सबैभन्दा धेरै संख्यामा प्रदुषित नदीहरू छन् र मानव मलबाट उत्पन्न हुने ब्याक्टेरियाको संख्या औसत भन्दा तीन गुणा बढी छ । संसारभरी प्रदुषित पानीको कारणले जलचर जीवको लोप हुने सम्भावना थलचरको भन्दा ५ गुणा बढी रहेको छ ।

This is a scene near the Goheshwori Temple of a painting event sponsored by the government to commemorate the 150th consecutive Saturday clean-up of the Bagmati River. Sixteen professional painters depicted their future dreams for the river.

Artists' dreams for the future of the Bagmati River

Ramesh Khanal

Shankar Raj Singh Suwal

Hari Khadka

Erina Tamrakar

Sunita Rana

Sanjay Bantawa

Kiran Manandhar

Krishna Manandhar

Raju Pithakote

Mahesh Acharya

Naresh Saiju

Surendra Pradhan

Dipendra Man Banepali

Jeevan Raj Padhaya

Shanta Kumar Rai

Devendra Thumkely

Shivapuri Nagarjun
National Park

Kathmandu

BAGMATI RIVER

Bhaktapur

Lalitpur

Nepal and Kathmandu Valley

The story of the Kathmandu Valley, which includes the cities of Kathmandu, Lalitpur, and Bhaktapur, started in 900 BC as a settlement along the Bagmati River that became the origin of Nepalese civilization. Over the centuries, many important Hindu and Buddhist temples where constructed that remain to this day. UNESCO (United Nations Educational, Scientific and Cultural Organization) has listed the entire valley as a "World Heritage Site" including seven individual UNESCO Heritage sites located within its borders. The importance of religion in everyday life is evident in the numerous small temples found in almost every block, and the inclusion of religious artifacts in every household and many doorways. Eighty percent of Nepalis practice Hinduism and 11 percent are Buddhist although both religions are intertwined and many temples are used by both religions. Hinduism is the oldest practiced religion with the third largest following worldwide. The majority of Hindus in the world live in India, which borders Nepal. The religion does not have any single founder but instead combines several different deities with many diverse rituals and gods based on nature. Buddhism follows the teachings of Buddha who was born in Nepal. Both religions strive for a sense of enlightenment and liberation from the material world as they yearn to connect with their spiritual identity. This selflessness is apparent in the residents of the Valley and becomes contagious to those who visit.

नेपाल र काठमाडौँ उपत्यका

काठमाडौँ उपत्यकाको इतिहाससँगै काठमाडौँ, ललितपुर र भक्तपुरको इतिहास जोडिएको छ र यसको सुरुआत १०० इसा पूर्व मा बागमती नदीको किनारमा नेपाली सभ्यताको सुरुआतसँगै भएको थियो । विभिन्न शताब्दीमा यहाँ धेरै हिन्दु तथा बौद्ध धार्मीक स्थलहरुको स्थापना गरियो जुन अहिले पनि देख्न पाइन्छ । युनेस्कोले उपत्यकालाई ने विश्व सम्पदाको सूचीमा र रखेको छ भने यसको सिमानाभित्र ७ वटा विश्व सम्पदाहरु रहेका छन् । हरेक चोकमा रहेका सानासाना मन्दिरहरु र हरेक घर र मूलढोकामा रहेका धार्मिक वस्तुहरुले यहाँ दैनिक जीवनमा धर्मको महत्व दर्शाउँछ । ८० प्रतिशत हिन्दु र ११ प्रतिशत बौद्ध धर्मावलम्बी रहेको यस देशमा दुवै धर्म एक आपसमा जोडिएका छन् र धेरै धार्मीक स्थल दुवै धर्मका श्रद्धालुहरुले मान्ने गरेको पाइन्छ । हिन्दु धर्म विश्वको सबैमन्दा पुरानो धर्म हो र तेस्रो सबैमन्दा धेरै धर्मावलम्बी भएको धर्म पनि हो । सबैमन्दा धेरै हिन्दुहरु नेपालको दक्षिणी छिमेकी भारतमा बसोबास गर्छन् । यस धर्मको कुनै एक प्रचारक नभई विभिन्न प्रकृति र रिति रिवाजसँग आवद्ध विभिन्न देवीदेवताहरु छन् । बौद्ध धर्म नेपालमा जन्मेका गौतम बुद्धका शिक्षामा आधारित छ । दुवै धर्म भौतिक संसारबाट मुक्ति र आध्यात्मको प्राप्तीका लागि प्रेरित गर्छन् । उपत्यकाका बासिन्दामा पनि यो निःस्वार्थ भाव पाउन सकिन्छ र यहाँ आउने आगन्तुक पनि यसबाट प्रभावित हुने गर्छन् ।

The country is eighty percent mountain and 20 percent plains and has 8 of the highest mountains in the world including Mt. Everest, which is 161 km (100 miles) from Kathmandu. It can take up to 9 days to walk from Everest base Camp (5,364m/ 17,598 ft) as you adjust to the elevation but only 4 days to return. The Himalayas, which Everest is part of, have the world's third largest deposit of ice behind the Artic and Antarctic. The abundance of hydroelectric power in Nepal's 6000 rivers is significant, and its potential continues to improve as climate changes increase the rate of melting glaciers and ice caps. If the country could tap these huge reserves it would provide more economic and agricultural stability as it has done for its neighboring countries, which have constructed hundreds of dams in the mountain range although at the cost of major environmental impact. Nepal, a poor country, has relied on foreign investment for major infrastructure projects, which has been difficult to secure due to instability and inefficiency in the government. Those that have been started have often been stalled or stopped due to governmental bureaucracy and red tape.

नेपालमा ८० प्रतिशत भूभाग हिमाल/पहाड र २० प्रतिशत तराई रहेको छ भने काठमाडौँबाट १६१ कि.मी. (१०० मिल) को दूरीमा अवस्थित सगरमाथा सहित विश्वका ८ सर्वोच्च शिखरहरु यहाँ छन् । हिँडेर सगर माथा बेस क्याम्प (५,३६४ मि/ १७, ५९८ फिट) पुग्न ९ दिनसम्म लाग्छ भने फर्किंदा मात्र ४ दिन लाग्छ । आर्टिक र अन्टार्टिक पछि विश्वमा सबैभन्दा धेरै हिउँ नेपालको हिमालयमा पाइन्छ । नेपालका ६००० नदीहरुमा जलविद्युतको प्रखर सम्भावना रहेको छ र हिमालयमा हिउँ पग्लिदैँ जाँदा यसको क्षमता झन बढेर गएको छ । नेपालसँग रहेको यो क्षमताको पूर्ण उपयोग गर्न सकेमा देशमा आर्थिक र कृषि क्षेत्रमा अझ बढी विकास गर्न सकिन्छ । छिमेकी राष्ट्रहरूले बाँध बनाएर यस क्षमताको लाभ उठाइरहेका छन् तर यसले वातावरणमा नराम्रो प्रभाव पारिरहेको छ । एक गरीब मुलुक नेपाल भौतिक विकासको लागि विदेशी लगानीमा भर पर्ने गरेको छ तर देशमा रहेको अस्थिरता र सरकारको अक्षमताले विदेशी लगानीकर्ताहरुलाई आकर्षित गर्न कठिन हुँदै गएको छ । विदेशी लगानीमा हुने धेरै योजनाहरु सरकार र प्रशासनले गर्दा कि त बन्द हुन बाध्य भएका छन् कि त बिचमै अड्किएका छन् ।

High up in the mountain near the Bagmati River in the Shivapuri Nagarjun National Park, you will find remnants of past pilgrimages.

Nepal is located between two much larger countries, China and India. Nepal's 3000 years of governance has been deeply affected by its relationship between these two powerful countries. There has been a long history of productivity, political change, and cultural developments mixed with bouts of unrest and instability. Its present structure is relatively young with its first official democratic constitution coming into effect in September of 2015. This constitution did not occur without controversy. Ethnic minorities, located along major trade checkpoints between India and Nepal, felt slighted by their representation in the new government and stopped shipments of food, fuel, medicine and other supplies. This disruption of supplies, which occurred after a series of devastating earthquakes and aftershocks starting in April of 2015, crippled the country. Strikes and protests continue to occur regularly as Nepal struggles with its new democratic government and as it continues to create stronger diplomatic relationship with its neighbors.

नेपाल दुई शक्तिशाली मुलुक भारत र चिनको बिचमा अवस्थित छ र नेपालको ३००० वर्ष देखिको सरकारतन्त्र यी दुई देशसँगको सम्बन्धबाट अत्यन्त प्रभावित हुने गरेको छ । नेपालको इतिहासमा भौतिक तथा सांस्कृतिक विकासको लामो अवधिसँगै समय समयमा अस्थिरता र अशान्ति पनि देख्न सकिन्छ । असोज २०७२ देखि सञ्चालनमा आएको नेपालको पहिलो गणतान्त्रिक संविधान प्रारंभिक चरणमै छ । यो संविधान बिना विवाद आएको होइन । भारत र नेपालको नाकामा बसोबास गर्ने अल्पसंख्यक समुदायहरुले यस संविधानबाट उपेक्षित महसूस गरेर खाद्य पदार्थ, ईंधन, औषधि तथा अन्य आवश्यक वस्तुको आपूर्ति अवरुद्ध गरिदिएका थिए । विनाशकारी भूकम्प र परकम्पको मारबाट गुज्रिरहेको नेपाललाई यो अवरोधले अझ ठूलो समस्यामा पारिदियो । नयाँ गणतान्त्रिक सरकारको सञ्चालन र छिमेकी राष्ट्रहरुसँगको सम्बन्ध सुधार्न संघर्षरत नेपालमा नियमित रुपमा बन्द र विरोध भइरहेको हुन्छ ।

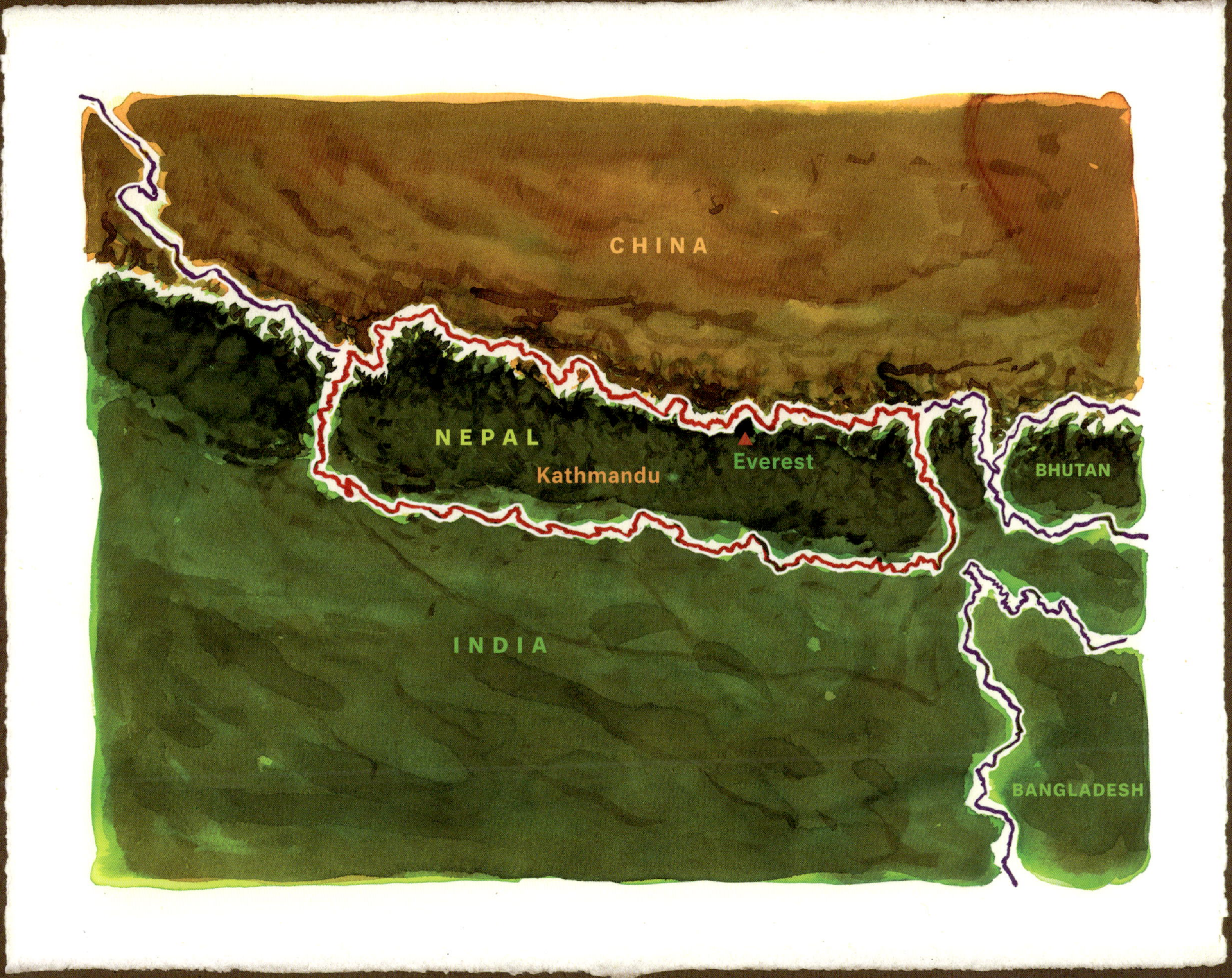

CHINA

NEPAL

Kathmandu

Everest

BHUTAN

INDIA

BANGLADESH

The instability in government for the last half century, new policies allowing unrestricted migration into Kathmandu since the 1950's, and the uncontrolled population and industrial growth in Kathmandu Valley since that period have all contributed to a complex set of circumstances that have nurtured a culture and environment where water and air pollution have grown to life-threatening levels. Half of the patients in some hospitals in Kathmandu are recovering from water-borne diseases while the other half are suffering from Chronic Obstructive Pulmonary Disease (COPD), a lung disease directly affected by air pollution. The extremely high levels of water and air pollution have provided Kathmandu with the inauspicious 2016 ranking as the third most polluted city in the world behind Tetovo City, Macedonia and Cairo, Egypt.

विगत आधि शताब्दीदेखि को सरकारी अस्थिरता, नयाँ निति जसले १९५० देखि काठमाडौँमा बेरोकटोक प्रवास र अनियंत्रित जनसंख्या वृद्धिको बाटो खोलिदियो र औद्योगिक विकासले काठमाडौँमा पानी र हावाको प्रदुषण घातक हुनपुगेको छ । काठमाडौँका केही अस्पतालहरुमा आधी दुषित पानीका बिरामीहरु छन् भने बाँकी प्रदुषित हावाले हुने फोक्सोको रोगका बिरामी छन् । हावा र पानीको उच्च प्रदुषणले काठमाडौँलाई मेसोडोनियाको तेतोभो सिटी र इजिप्टको कायरो शहर पछि २०१६ को सबैभन्दा प्रदुषित शहरको सूचीमा तेस्रो नम्बरमा पुर्‍याएको छ ।

This is the front page from the Kathmandu Post March 19th, 2016.

the kathmandu post | 02

Kathmandu 3rd most polluted city in the world

BREATHING IN DIRTY AIR

Rank	City	Pollution Index
1	Tetovo, Macedonia	99.24
2	Cairo, Egypt	99.10
3	Kathmandu, Nepal	96.66
4	Accra, Ghana	96.18
5	Manila, Philippines	96.08
6	Noida, India	95.55
7	Guangzhou, China	94.66
8	Delhi, India	94.14
9	Ho Chi Minh City, Vietnam	94.00
10	Alexandria, Egypt	93.99

POST REPORT
KATHMANDU, MARCH 19

In a latest finding which may not surprise many, Kathmandu has been ranked the third most polluted city in the world.

According to Pollution Index 2016 published by Ministry of Science, Technology and Environment, showing Kathmandu air contains 400 micrograms of particulate matter up to 10 micrometres in size per cubic metre or the PM10 is 400µg/m3–over three-fold the permissible limits. The maximum limit set by the National Ambient Air Quality Standards for PM10 is per litre or the DO is 0.50mg/l. No aquatic animal can survive in water with less than 3mg/l. Likewise, chemical oxygen demand of water (total measurement of all chemicals in the water that can be oxidised) at the same place was 138.04mg/l and biochemical oxygen demand (the amount of dissolved oxygen needed by aerobic biological

There has been a great deal of potential for economic and environmental rejuvenation that would match the rich cultural reserves that the Kathmandu Valley possesses. As many reports over the past decades have stated, the reality of addressing its present condition is complicated by the government's lack of collaboration, duplication of services, lack of direction, lack of financial resources and inability to tackle the complexities of its most difficult problems.

आर्थिक र वातावरणिय सम्पन्नताका लागि प्रशस्त आधार रहेपनि सरकारको असहयोग, दूरदर्शी नेतृत्वको अभाव, आर्थिक स्रोतको कमी, र समस्याको समाधान खोज्न सक्ने क्षमताको अभावले यो सफल हुनसकेको छैन ।

From Swayambhunath, a sacred Buddhist UNESCO Heritage Site on a mountain top, are panoramic views of Kathmandu and the layer of smog that often obscures the Himalayan Mountains that lie behind the city.

At Swayambhunath, similar to many other temples, there are weathered remnants of past decades.

While walking the streets in the evening in Patan, we often had to dodge oncoming motorcycles and cars on narrow ancient streets.

The Bagmati River in Kathmandu Valley

The sacred Bagmati River is where civilization began in Nepal. The river with its 20 tributaries and the fertile land in the basin, surrounded by the Mahabharat Mountain Range, is all that remains of an ancient lake from 30,000 years ago. Kathmandu, and with it the beginning of Nepalese culture and religion, was started along its banks. Ancient Hindu Sanskrit documents from the sixth century outline the origins of the river. The text describes a disciple going high into a mountain and performing religious rituals for a thousand years as a way to show his gratitude for the gods' assistance during a battle with a demon. Lord Shiva, one of the three major deities in Hinduism, was so happy with his dedication, "that the blooming laughter that rolled out of his mouth, took the form of an unsullied river, swirling with sacred water and whitened by garlands of foamy waves, arising and flowing forth out of the mouth of the cave in the mountains." Shiva declares that since the river was created from his voice that its name will be Vigmati (filled with the Voice). He also stipulates that this location will be a holy place for Hindus and that the headwaters of the river will be a prosperous place named Shivapuri (Shiva-town). He also proclaims that anyone who bathes and prays here will be absolved from all sins committed in present or previous lives.

काठमाडौँ उपत्यकामा बागमाती नदी

नेपालमा मानव सभ्यताको सुरुआत बागमती नदीकै किनारबाट भएको थियो । ३०,००० वर्ष पुरानो यस ऐतिहासिक तालको अहिले महाभारत पर्वत शृंखलाले धेरिएको बागमती नदी र यसका २० सहायक नदीहरु र उर्वर किनार मात्र देख्न सकिन्छ । काठमाडौँका साथै यसको संस्कृति र धर्मको सुरुआत बागमतीको किनारमे भएको हो । छैठौँ शताब्दीदेखि का प्राचीन संस्कृत दस्तावेजहरुमा नदीको उत्पति बारे लेखिएको छ । दस्तावेज अनुसार एक जना अनुयायीले एक दानवसँगको युद्धमा देवताले गरेको सहयोगप्रति आभार प्रकट गर्न हिमालयमा गई हजारौँ वर्षसम्म अनुष्ठान गरेको उल्लेख छ । हिन्दु धर्मका तीन देवमध्ये भगवान शिव उक्त अनुयायीको समर्पणबाट अत्यन्त प्रसन्न भए र उहाँको मुखबाट प्रस्फुटित हाँसोले एक अनियन्त्रित नदीको रुप लियो । शिवको स्वरबाट उत्पन्न भएकोले हिमालयमा रहेको गुफाबाट निस्किएको पवित्र पानी र सेतो माला जस्तै फिज भएको उक्त नदीको नाम शीवले भीग्मती (स्वरले भरिएको) राखे । शिवले उक्त नदी बग्ने स्थल हिन्दुहरुको पवित्र स्थल हुने र नदीको स्रोत एक समृद्ध ठाउँ हुनेछ र त्यसको नाम शिवपुरी (शिवको शहर) हुनेछ भनी उद्घोष गरे । शिवले यस नदीमा नुहाउँदा यस जन्मका साथै पूर्व जन्मको पापबाट पनि मुक्ति प्राप्त हुने पनि भने ।

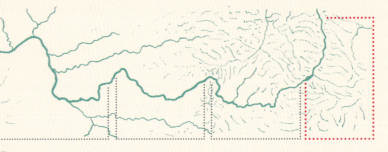

At the entrance of the Shivapuri Nagarjun, National Park, this maps provides a bit of guidance for trekking.

Shivapuri National Park

Kholegoun

Thanapati Sunkhani Sikre

Haibung

Chapgaun Rolche Chisapani

Alche Chitra Bha

Pateshowor Shivapuri park (2932 m.)

Kakani Panimuhan Taulung Mulkharka Dhaap

Dhokalchoun Budhanilkantha Tarebhir

Jagat Sangla Jhor Chapli Goun Phensechaun

Kabrasthali Balua

Lipikot Tokha Mahenkal Sundarijal Kurinkal Jhule

Jitpunphedi Dharmathali Futung Nayanpati

Manamaiju Jitpurphedi Sundarijal Laptiphedi

Dhapasi Chunikhel Manichaun

Kaghi

Mahankhani Danchi

| upto 2000m | | Piligrimages Site |
| above 2000m | | Main Trail |

Registered water tankers are one of the few sources of safe, drinkable water in the Kathmandu Valley. Many unregistered tankers, however, are not reliable.

Today you can find the origins of the Bagmati River as a small trickle in the dry season 2372 meters (7782 feet) high on the south face of Shivapuri Mountain in Baghdwar in the Shivapuri Nagarjun National Park. The location is marked by a densely forested narrow valley with hundreds of prayer flags draped between the trees. Small tributaries and springs add to the stream as it drops 700 meters (2300 feet) down to the Sundarijal Dam. Upstream of the dam, small villages located along the steep deforested hillside begin the river's degradation as their sewage is deposited into the water. During the dry season, 80 million liters a day (MLD) of this tainted water flows downhill to a water treatment plant built in 1966 before it is distributed to the 3 million residents in the Kathamandu Valley. During the wet season, this amount increases to 140 MLD but 36 percent of all the water is lost in old leaking pipes. The valley also has a plethora of leaking sewage lines, which contaminate the tap water with sewage seeping into the cracked water lines. The leaks in the water pipes bring the water totals reaching the residents down to 51 MLD and 86 MLD but the city needs 400 MLD. These totals have been further reduced due to the recent earthquake, which further damaged the water and sewage pipes and connections to springs and the valley's groundwater. The Kathmandu government has not been able to provide enough water for its growing population for decades, and there are times when the people have to wait for two weeks before they receive any tap water. The residents look to other options to fulfill their basic needs. These include using century old public spouts, drilling wells into the valley's groundwater, or purchasing water from tankers or bottled water vendors.

शिवपुरी पहाडको दक्षिणतरि बाघद्वारस्थित शिवपुरी नागार्जुन राष्ट्र निकुञ्जमा अहिले २३७२ मिटर (७७८२ फिट) को उचाईमा बागमती नदीको मूल रहेको छ । त्यहाँ वरिपरि घना जङ्गलका बिच रहेको सानो उपत्यकामा रुखहरुमा सयौं प्रार्थना ध्वज देख्न सकिन्छ । साना सहायक नदी र खोलाहरु मिसिँदै ७०० मिटर (२३०० फिट) तल झरेर सुन्दरिजल बाँधमा मिसिन्छ । सुन्दरीजलभन्दा माथि जाँदा बाँध किनारमा केही बस्तीहरु छन् जसबाट आएका ढलहरु यही खोलामा मिसिन्छन् र नदीको प्रदुषण यहीँबाट सुरु हुन्छ । सुक्खा याममा ८०० लाख लिटर प्रदुषित पानी १९६६ मा बनेको प्रशोधन केन्द्रमा संकलन हुन्छ र प्रशोधन पश्चात काठमाडौं उपत्यकाका ३० लाख बासिन्दालाई वितरण गरिन्छ । वर्षा याममा यो पानीको मात्रा बढेर १४०० लाख लिटर पुग्छ तर ३६ प्रतिशत पानी पुरानो पाइपहरुबाट चुहिएर जान्छ । उपत्यकामा ढलका पाइपहरु चुहिएर पनि खानेपानिमा मिसिने गर्दछ । पानी चुहिने समस्याले बासिन्दाहरुसम्म मात्र ५२० र ८६० लाख लिटर पानी पुग्ने गर्दछ जबकी खानेपानीको माग ४००० लाख लिटर रहेको छ । भुकम्प पछि पानी र ढलका पाइपहरुमा क्षति पुगेर पानीको आपूर्तिमा थप समस्या आएको छ । सरकारले काठमाडौंमा खानेपानीको पर्याप्त आपूर्ती गर्न सकेका छैन र कहिलेकहिले त हप्तौंसम्म पनि धारामा पानी आउँदैन । खानेपानीका लागि काठमाडौंका बासिन्दा ढुङ्गेधारा, इनार वा ट्याइकर वा बोतलको पानी खरिद गर्ने जस्ता अन्य विकल्प खोज्न बाध्य छन् ।

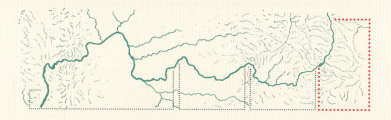

Another measure that the government has been working on since 2003 has been to increase the water volume to the city through the Melamchi Water Supply Project. This project has been delayed for several years, but the first phase of the project is expected to be completed by 2017. At a cost of 27 billion rupees (US $2.5 billion), it is financed mainly by the Asian Development Bank (ADB), which is a financial institution started in the mid 1960's to address poverty in Asia and the Pacific. The first phase of the project includes building a 26.5 kilometer (16.4 mile) tunnel that will bring an additional 170 MLD of water from the Melamchi River in Ribarma to a new water treatment plant near Sundarijal. Initially the water treatment plant will only be able to handle half of the new water supply from Melamchi. The new water will be transported to the valley through the existing damaged water pipes until new lines are put in. The other half of the water will be deposited in the Bagmati River. In time, a new water treatment plant will be able to handle 510MLD.

सन् २००३ देखि उपत्यकामा पानीको आपूर्ती सहज पार्न सरकारले मेलम्चीबाट पानी ल्याउने प्रयास गरिरहेको छ । धेरै वर्षदेखि चलिरहेको यस परियोजनाको पहिलो चरण २०१७ सम्म मा सकिने अनुमान गरिएको छ । एसिया तथा प्यासिफिक क्षेत्रको गरिबी निवारणलाई लक्षित गरी सन् १९६० मा स्थापना गरिएको एसिया विकास बैंक २७ खर्ब लागत रहेको यस परियोजनाको मुख्य वितिय साझेदार रहेको छ । परियोजनाको पहिलो चरणमा रिबर्मस्थित मेलम्ची नदीबाट सुन्दरीजलमा रहेको प्रशोधन केन्द्रमा १७०० लाख लिटर पानी ल्याउन २६.५ किलोमिटर लामो सुरुङ्ग निर्माण गर्ने योजना छ । सुरुआतमा मेलम्चीबाट आउने पानीको मात्र आधी पानी उक्त केन्द्रमा प्रशोधन गर्ने क्षमता रहेको छ । प्रशोधित पानीलाई नयाँ पाइपहरू नबिछ्याइएसम्म पुराने पाइपबाट उपत्यकाका घरघरमा पुऱ्याइनेछ । बाँकी पानी बागमती नदीमा छोडिनेछ । साथै १५०० लाख लिटर क्षमता भएको एक नयाँ प्रशोधन केन्द्र निर्माण गर्ने योजना पनि छ । दोस्रो चरण अन्तर्गत खानेपानी संस्थाले पोलिइथाइलिनका उच्च घनत्वका ७०० किलोमिटर पाइपहरू बिछाउनेछ । नयाँ पाइपलाइनले पानी चुहिने समस्यालाई न्यून पार्ने अनुमान गरिए पनि उक्त पाइपलाइन पूर्ण रूपमा सञ्चालनमा आउन अझ ५७ वर्ष लाग्नेछ । यस चरणमा शहर

Phase 1
Melamchi Tunnel

Phase 2

Sundarijal

MELAMCHI RIVER

Kathmandu Valley

BAGMATI RIVER

The second phase of the project involves having the Kathmandu Valley's water department putting in 700km (435 miles) of high-density polyethylene water pipe around the city, which will then connect to households and businesses. This new pipeline will drastically reduce leakage, but it will take 5 to 7 years to be completely operational. This phase also includes creating six new water reservoirs around the city and increasing the volume of new water an additional 170MLD from the Larke and Yangri Rivers in the Melamchi Valley. In time, the plan is to increase the total volume to 510 MLD and create new sewage treatment plants. While it would have been sensible to have the new water lines and reservoirs finished by the time the tunnel was completed, it was not possible because of the financial costs. If all of the 510 MLD of water from the project becomes available and the sewage treatment plants are built, it would reduce the withdrawal and use of water from the valley's groundwater. The groundwater is currently being depleted quicker than it can be restored and is also contaminated with high levels of arsenic, ammonia, iron nitrates and E. coli bacteria. However, as has been the case in the past, earthquakes, political conflicts with neighboring countries, and ineffective government services could derail the true potential of the project's capacity.

परिपरि थप ६ वटा जलाशयको निर्माण गरी लार्की र याङ्ग्री नदीबाट १७०० लाख लिटर पानी मेलम्चीमा थप्ने योजना पनि छ । साथै समयसँगै कूल ५१०० लाख लिटर पानी आपूर्ती गर्ने र नयाँ ढल निकासको निर्माण गर्ने योजना पनि रहेको छ । सुरुङ्ग बन्नु अगावै नयाँ पाइपलाइन र ढलको निर्माण भइसक्नुपर्ने भएपनि आर्थिक कारणले यो सम्भव हुन सकेन । ५१०० लाख लिटर पानी आपूर्ती गर्ने र नयाँ ढल निर्माण गर्ने योजना सफल भयो भने जमिनमुनिको पानीमाथिको निर्भरता अन्त्य हुनेछ । जमिनमुनीको पानी अहिले तिव्र गतिमा घट्नुका साथै यसमा आर्सेनिक, अमोनिया, आइरन नाइट्रेट र इ कोलाइ ब्याक्टेरिया जस्ता हानिकारक तत्व अत्याधिक मात्रामा छन् । तथापि विगतमा जस्तै भुकम्प, छिमेकी राष्ट्रसँगको सम्बन्धमा तिक्तता र सरकारी असमर्थताले परियोजनाको क्षमतमा ह्रास ल्याउन सक्ने सम्भावना पनि छ ।

Neighborhood gardens in Gokarneswor on the outskirts of Kathmandu are irrigated using toxic Bagmati River water.

At the Sundarijal Dam, around 86 percent of the river's water is diverted to a hydro-electric plant and then to its water treatment plant. The Bagmati River immediately gets further degraded as it leaves the Shivapuri Nagarjun National Park. Sewer lines flow directly into the river from the densely packed settlements that line the cement path to the park. The river flows south toward Gokarna, which was once the capital of Nepal before it was moved to Patan in 75 BC, located across the river from present day Kathmandu. The elevation continues to drop a few hundred meters as the river picks up sewage and industrial, farm and hospital waste from the Syalmati and Kolmati Rivers. The sand in the river helps to filter some of the waste but it can not keep up with the contaminated water. On the banks of the river near a pass in the mountain range, the Gokarna Mahadev temple, built in 1582, stands and is an important site for religious rituals and pilgrimages during Hindu father's day in late August - early September. Downstream of the temple, there's a small pass through the mountain that leads into the valley. At the base of the pass is a small dam with a series metal gates that control the Bagmati River during the wet season. Below the gates, it is common to see the residents of southern Gokarneswor washing their clothes against the exposed rocks, bathing in the slow currents of the polluted river and using the water to irrigate their crops that are planted along the riverbank.

सुन्दरीजल बाँधमा ८६ प्रतिशतभन्दा बढी पानी जलविद्युत परियोजना र त्यसपछि प्रशोधन केन्द्रमा पठाइन्छ । शिवपुरी नागार्जुन पार्कबाट बाहिर निस्केपछि बागमति नदी अझ प्रदुषित हुनपुग्छ । पार्कका वरिपरिका घना बस्तीबाट ढल सोझै नदीमा मिसिन्छ । नदी त्यसपछि दक्षिण दिशातर्फ बग्दै गोकर्ण पुग्छ । ७५ इसा पूर्वमा पाटन सार्नुभन्दा अगाडी गोकर्ण नेपालको राजधानी हुने गर्थ्यो । नदी अझ केही सय मिटर तलतिर बग्दै गर्दा यसमा स्यालमती र कोलमतिस्थित कलकारखाना र अस्पतालबाट निस्किने फोहोर पनि मिसिने गर्छ । नदीमा रहेको बालुवाले केही हदसम्म पानी प्रशोधन गरेपनि यो पर्याप्त हुँदैन । नदी किनारमा रहेको पहाड शृंखलामा एक भन्ज्याङमा सन् १५८२ मा निर्मित गोकर्ण महादेवको मन्दिर रहेको छ । हिन्दु धर्ममा खासगरी बुआको मुख हेर्ने दिनमा यस मन्दिरको खास महत्व रहेको छ । मन्दिरबाट अझ तलतिर एउटा भन्ज्याङ उपत्यकासम्म पुग्दछ । भन्ज्याङको बेसीमा शृंखलाबद्ध रुपमा रहेका फलामे ढोकाहरुले वर्षा याममा बागमती नदीको बहावलाई नियंत्रित गर्छन् । उक्त ढोकाहरुभन्दा तलतिर गोकर्णेश्वरका बासिन्दाहरुले नदी किनारका ढुङ्गामा लुगा धोएको, प्रदुषित पानीमा नुहाएको र उक्त पानीले सिंचाई गरेको दृश्य देख्न सकिन्छ ।

Below the flood gates on the Bagmati River near Gokarna, residents bathe and wash clothes in highly contaminated water.

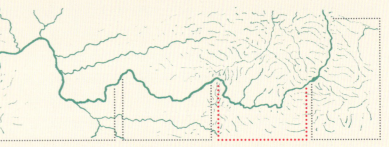

The river runs straight for about a mile before it flows into several oxbows leading to the northeastern edge of city of Kathmandu. Along one major bend in the river are two of the holiest Hindu temples in Nepal. The first is Guhyeshwari Temple, which was built in the 17th century and is located across the river from the only working sewage treatment plant in the valley. The plant only works when electricity is available, which in the dry season can be as infrequent as half the day. It services only 1,500 out of the 400,000 households in the city. Large sewage pipes are visible near the holy temple, which continue to pollute the sacred site. Just downstream and around the bend is the Pashupatinath Temple, which is one of the seven UNESCO World Heritage Sites in the valley. The entire hillside between Pashupatinath and Guhyeshwari is dotted with many temples and families of monkeys interspersed between the buildings. The temple complex receives up to 700,000 Hindus during religious pilgrimage holidays and is regularly the site of funeral pyres for loved ones. While bathing in the river is an important part of the rituals, most no longer feel safe to enter the river due to its polluted state and the river's cultural significance is diminished with each passing generation.

करिब २ कोषसम्म सिधा बगेपछि नदीमा धेरै मोडहरु आउँछन् । यस्तै एउटा मोडमा हिन्दुहरुको अत्यन्त पवित्र मन्दिरहरु रहेका छन् । पहिलो मन्दिर हो गुहेश्वरी जसको निर्माण १७ औँ शताब्दीमा भएको थियो र यो उपत्यकाको एकमात्र परिचालित ढल व्यवस्थापन केन्द्र नजिक रहेको छ । ढल व्यवस्थापन बत्ती भएको बेला मात्र काम गर्छ र सुक्खा याममा बत्ती मात्र दिनको १२ घण्टासम्म हुनसक्छ । ४००,००० मध्ये मात्र १,५०० घरहरु यस केन्द्रसँग जोडिएका छन् । मन्दिर नजिकै ढलका ठूला पाइपहरु देख्न सकिन्छन् जसले यस पवित्र स्थललाई प्रदूषित गरिरहेका छन् । अझ तलतिर जाँदा अर्को मोडमा पशुपतिनाथ मन्दिर रहेको छ । पशुपतिनाथ युनेस्कोको विश्व सम्पदाको सूचीमा रहेका ७ सम्पदामध्ये एक हो । गुहेश्वरी र पशुपतिबिचका डाँडाहरु ससाना मन्दिरहरु र बाँदरहरुले भरिएको छन् । विभिन्न हिन्दु चाडहरुमा पशुपतिनाथमा कूल ७००,००० सम्म श्रद्धालुहरु आउने गर्छन् । साथै पशुपतिको घाटमा नियमित दाह संस्कार पनि हुने गर्छ । पशुपतिको नदीमा नुहाउनु एक महत्वपूर्ण धार्मिक प्रक्रिया भएपनि नदीमा बढ्दै गएको प्रदुषणले गर्दा श्रद्धालु अहिले नदीमा जानुमा संकोच मान्छन् र हरेक पुस्तासँगै नदीको सांस्कृतिक महत्व घट्दै गएको छ ।

1:36 pm - Guhesuni, Kathmandu, Nepal - March 18, 2016

The Bagmati becomes even more contaminated as it flows downstream past squatter settlements and worsens when the Manohora River joins it. The river flows through dense neighborhoods separating Kathmandu from Patan. The river emits a malodorous smell as it is joined by yet, another contaminated tributary, the Dhobi River. More temporary settlements are found downstream. These settlements, like the rest of the region, deposit their liquid and solid waste directly into the river. Kathmandu is currently looking for a new landfill site to deposit the 992 tons of garbage collected daily, which constitutes only 70% of the solid waste in the city. The garbage includes infectious and hazardous waste mixed with general garbage. Until a site is selected, some municipalities have recommended that the garbage be left on the banks of the Bagmati River. Many years ago, this section was destined to be a United Nations Park but the vision was never realized. Further south, the Bagmati is joined with the polluted waters from the Tukucha and Bishnumati Rivers. Near Tribhuvan University, heaps of garbage can be seen along the river as local municipalities dump around 25 trucks of garbage on the banks of the river daily. As the river reaches the end of the Kathmandu Valley, it meets with two more polluted tributaries, the Balkhu River and Nakhu River. The Bagmati's volume has continued to increase with each tributary it meets, so by the time it exits the valley through a pass in the surrounding mountain range, it is running high and black with sewage and industrial waste.

सुकुम्बासी बस्तीको छेउबाट बग्दै गरेर मनहरा नदीसँग मिसिदासम्म बागमती अझ प्रदुषित हुन पुग्छ । बागमती त्यसपछि काठमाडौँ र पाटनको सिमामा रहेको घना बस्तीको बिचबाट बग्दै जान्छ । बहावको क्रममा नदी अन्य बस्तीहरुबाट गुज्रिन्छ । यी बस्तीका बासिन्दाहरुले पनि आफ्ना फोहोर नदीमै फाल्ने गर्छन् । अहिले काठमाडौँमा दैनिक ९९२ टन फोहोर, जुन कूल सुक्खा फोहोर मैलाको मात्र ७० प्रतिशत हुन आउँछ, को व्यवस्थापनका लागि नयाँ जमिनको खोजी हुँदैछ । सामान्य फोहोरसँगै यसमा हानीकारक र संक्रमण फैलाउने तत्वहरु पनि रहेका हुन्छन् । नयाँ ठाउँको व्यवस्था नभएसम्म नगरपालिकाले फोहोर बागमतीको किनारमा फाल्ने सुझाव दिएको छ । केही वर्ष अगाडी बागमती किनारमा संयुक्त राष्ट्र (यूएन) को पार्क बनाउने योजना रहेपनि यसले पूर्णता पाउन सकेको छैन । अझ दक्षिणतिर पुग्दा बागमतीमा टुकुचा र विष्णुमतीका फोहोर पानी मिसिन पुग्छन् । त्रिभुवन विश्वविद्यालय नजिकै नगरपालिकाले दैनिक २५ ट्रक फोहोर फाल्ने गरेकोले त्यहाँ फोहोरको ठूलो थुप्रो नै रहेको छ । काठमाडौँको अन्त्यसम्म पुग्दा बागमतीमा अझ २ प्रदुषित नदी बल्खु र नक्खु मिसिने गर्छन् । बागमतीको पानी हरेक सहायक नदीसँगको संगमसँगै बढ्दै जान्छ र उपत्काबाट बाहिरिदासम्म यसको पानी ढल र फोहोरले कालो भइसककेको हुन्छ ।

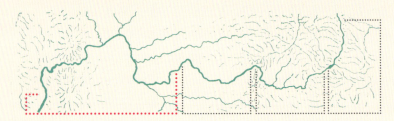

Video still illustrates the Bagmati's sewage-laden black water at Chovar.

A music video is filmed on the banks of the Bagmati River in front of the Jal Binayak Temple at Chovar.

At Chovar, the river suddenly slows down and widens into a plain that is littered with garbage, visible far into the smog-laden horizon. On the day we visited there was a camera crew filming a music video of a thin, young, attractive singer in a long reflective blue silk dress standing on a boulder. Just out of camera shot, at the feet of the singer, were piles of garbage. In the background was the Jal Binayak Temple, a four hundred year-old structure dedicated to Ganesh, one of the most worshipped Hindu deities. Just outside the temples walls, a middle-aged man squatted next to the body of a recently sacrificed goat. In his left hand was a small propane torch whose flame slowly moved over the charred severed head. In the distance, we could hear the young song-stress. Her song was hauntingly beautiful.

चोभार पुग्दा बागमतीको बहाव अचानक थामिन्छ र नदी समतल क्षेत्रमा प्रवेश गर्छ जहाँ जताततै फोहोरहरु फालिएका छन् । हामी त्यहाँ गएको दिन रेशमी पहिरणमा सजिएकी एक आकर्षक गायिकाको म्यूजिक भिडियोको शुटिङ भइरहेको थियो । क्यमेराको क्षेत्रमन्दा बाहिर गायिकाको खुट्टा नजिकै फोहोरको थुप्रो थियो । पृष्ठभूमीमा भगवान गणेशको ४०० वर्ष पुरानो मन्दिर जलविणायक थियो । मन्दिर परिसरमन्दा ठीक बाहिर एक जना मान्छे बली चढाइएको खसी अगाडी बसेर टर्चको उज्यालोमा खसीको टाउको नियालिरहेका थिए । परबाट ती गायिकाको सुमधुर आवाज आइरहेको थियो । उनले गाइरहेको गीत अत्यन्त मर्मस्पर्शी थियो ।

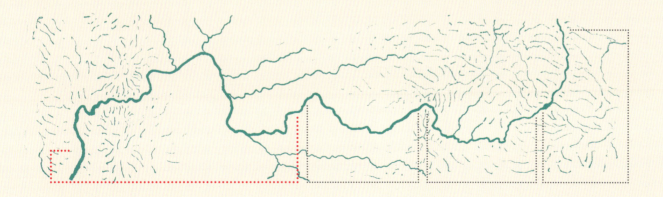

Highly decorated buses often park near Yalamaya in Patan.

Doorways, like this one in Kathmandu Durbar Square, often have a collection of bent nails pounded into the wood to keep demons from entering the building.

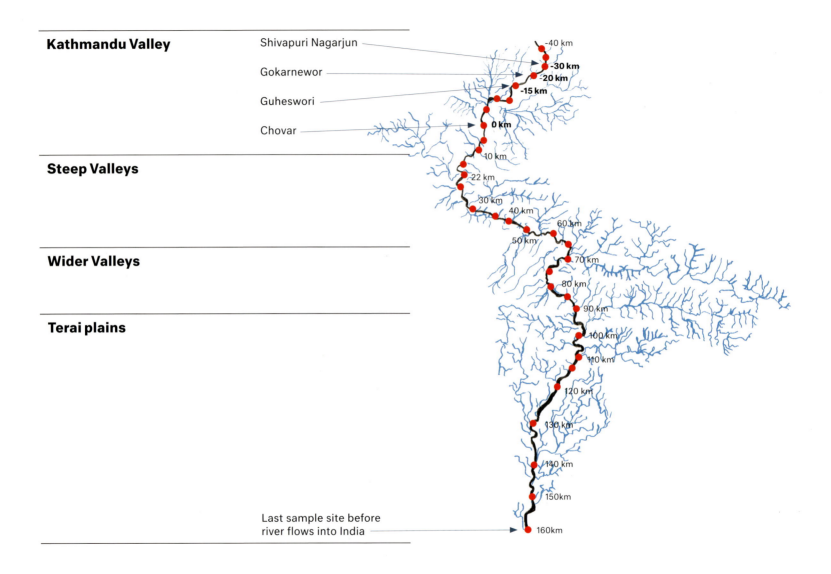

Kathmandu Valley

Shivapuri Nagarjun

Gokarnewor

Guheswori

Chovar

Steep Valleys

Wider Valleys

Terai plains

-40 km

-30 km

-20 km

-15 km

0 km

10 km

22 km

30 km

40 km

60 km

50 km

70 km

80 km

90 km

100 km

110 km

120 km

130 km

140 km

150km

Last sample site before
river flows into India

160km

Bagmati River Expedition 2015

Fortunately for our project, the Bagmati River Expedition 2015 occurred a few months before our trip to Nepal. We had carefully studied the expedition report (http://biosphereassociation.org/uploads/3/1/4/1/3141117/fullreportbre2015.pdf) before arriving in Kathmandu and were able to meet and interview a few of the scientists who were responsible for the venture. The Bagmati River Expedition 2015 research of the entire river was conducted in two parts. From April 12-23, 2015, the expedition studied the river from Chovar to the edge of the Nepalese border at Gaur where the river flows into India and ultimately joins the Ganges River, which flows into the Bay of Bengal and then the Indian Ocean. The first part of the expedition finished two days before the April 25 earthquake that devastated the country. The team conducted the second part of the expedition between Chovar and the river's source at Baghdwar from June 3rd to July 3rd. The team hiked most of the 200 Km (124 miles) and collected samples every 5 km (3 miles). At each site, they studied water volume, water chemistry, the bacteria levels, plastics on the banks, insect populations in the water, nearby bird populations, water use, sanitation and flooding.

बागमती नदी यात्रा २०१५

भाग्यवस हामी काठमाडौं आउनुभन्दा केही महीना अगाडी नै बागमती नदी यात्रा २०१५ भएको थियो । यहाँ आउनुभन्दा अगाडी हामी ले यस यात्राको प्रतिवेदन (http://biosphereassociation.org/uploads/3/1/4/1/3141117/fullreportbre2015.pdf) पढेका थियौं र यसमा संलग्न केही वैज्ञानिकलाई भेटेर कुरा पनि गरेका थियौं । बागमती नदी यात्राका क्रममा दुइ चरणमा बागमती नदीमाथि शोध गरिएको थियो । अप्रिल १२१४, २०१५ सम्म चोभारदेखि नेपालको सिमानामा रहेको गौरसम्मको अध्ययन गरिएको थियो जहाँबाट नदी भारत प्रवेश गर्छ र गंगा नदीमा मिसिन्छ जो बँगालको खाडी हुँदै हिन्द महासागरमा गएर मिसिन्छ । पहिलो चरणको यात्रा महाभूकम्पको २ दिन अगाडी सकेको थियो । जून ३ देखि जुलाई ३ सम्म उक्त समूहले चोभारदेखि बागमती नदीको मूल रहेको बाघद्वारसम्मको अध्ययन गर्यो । शोधकर्ताको समूहले २०० किलोमिटरको उक्त यात्रा धेरैजसो हिँडेर तय गर्यो र हरेक ५ किलोमिटरको दूरीमा पानीको नमूना पनि संकलन गर्यो । प्रत्येक स्थलमा तिनीहरुले पानीको मात्रा, पानीको रसायन, ब्याक्टेरियाको मात्रा, किनारमा रहेको प्लास्टिक, पानीमा रहेको जीवको संख्या, नजिकैको चराहरुको जनसंख्या, पानीको उपयोग, सरसफाइ र बाढीको अध्ययन गरे ।

Colony Counts (log10) per 1ml of sample

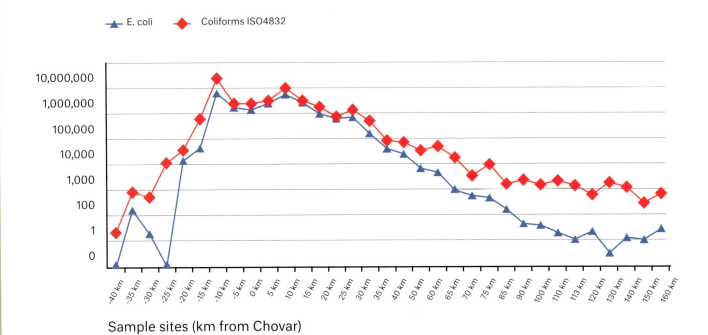

Sample sites (km from Chovar)

Nepal Guidelines colony count per 100ml	Drinking water	Recreation full contact	Recreation partial contact	Water for animals	Irrigation	Irrigation where edible parts are not wetted
E. coli	0	< 130	-	-	-	-
Fecal Coliform	-	< 130	< 1000	< 200	< 1	1–1000

Colony counts per 1ml of sample for coliform and E. coli along the Bagmati River
with the Nepalese water quality guidelines for *E. coli* fecal coliform for different water uses.
Bagmati River Expedition 2015:

Their most troubling conclusions concerned the bacteria count in the river. Their data indicated that the river's water was safe to drink only at its source in Baghdwar. Just 5km (3miles) downstream at -35km site, the bacteria count begins to spike as the river passes below a few small villages on the steep hillside along the river's banks. While still inside the Shivapuri Nagarjun National Park and upstream from where the valley collects its drinking water, Escherichia coli (E. Coli) levels raise to 10 colony counts per milliliter (0.2 teaspoon). Safe drinking water should not have any E. Coli. This bacteria is found in the feces of warm blooded animals like humans and is an indication of the presence of fecal material in the water. It can also predict the presence of disease-carrying-bacteria. Because of the high levels of bacteria in the water in the valley, water- borne diseases such as diarrhea, dysentery, cholera and various skin disease are common in Kathmandu Valley.

प्राप्त जानकारीमध्ये सबैभन्दा चिंतित बनाउने नदीमा रहेको ब्याक्टेरियाको संख्या थियो । तीनीहरूले प्राप्त गरेका तथ्याङ्क अनुसार नदीको मूल बाघद्वारको पानी मात्र खान योग्य थियो । मात्र ५ किलोमिटर तल पुगेपछि साना गाउँहरूसम्म पुग्दा ब्याक्टेरियाको संख्या उच्च हुनथाल्छ । नागार्जुन राष्ट्रिय निकुञ्जमा जहाँबाट उपत्यकामा खानेपानी आउँछ इ.कोलाईको मात्रा प्रति मिलिलिटर १० कोलोनि काउन्ट (जीवाणु गणना गर्ने एकाइ) रहेको पता लाग्यो । खानेपानीमा इ. कोलाइ हुनुहुँदैन । यो ब्याक्टेरिया मानिसजस्तै अन्य स्तनपायी जीवको मलमा पाइने गर्छ र यो ब्याक्टेरिया पाउनुले पानीमा मल मिसिएको संकेत गर्नुका साथै रोग पैदा गर्ने ब्याक्टेरियाको उपस्थितिको सम्भावना पनि दर्शाउँछ । उपत्यकाको पानीमा ब्याक्टेरियाको उच्च संख्या भएकोले उपत्यकामा झाडापखाला, हैजा तथा विभिन्न चर्म रोग फैलिने गरेको छ ।

From this point (-35) downstream, the river's water is not only unsafe to drink, but is also unfit for use in irrigating edible plants although many residents use the river to water their crops. This continued practice indicates the need to increase awareness of how toxic levels of chemicals in the water can damage the soil and using the polluted water can transmit dangerous bacteria into the food chain. The contaminated soil can have the longest potential to harbor these disease-carrying bacteria. The river's water is also unsafe for "full contact" once the river leaves the national park (-30) and remains that way until 85 km (53 miles) downstream after it leaves the Kathmandu Valley. "Full contact" refers to a significant or lengthy full immersion of a body, for example, swimming or bathing. The water is also unsafe for "partial contact" once it reaches the valley (-25) around Gokarna just a few kilometers from the national park. It remains in this condition until 75 km (47 miles) downstream of when the river flows past Chovar. "Partial contact" refers to a brief immersion of the body or splashing. All along the river in the valley where the water is only partially stained and does not provide a visual indication that anything is wrong, we witnessed residents bathing and washing clothes while the children played in the water and dug in the sewage-laden mud for bugs.

यो बिन्दु (३५) बाट तल पानी खानको लागि मात्र नभइ सिंचाइको लागि पनि अयोग्य छ तर उपत्यकामा सिंचाईका लागि बागमतीको पानी प्रयोग गर्नु सामान्य रहेको छ । यस विषादीयुक्त पानीले माटोमा गर्ने हानी र रोग फैलाउने जीवाणु सार्न सक्ने खतरा बारे जनमानसमा जागरुकता फैलाउने आवश्यकता देखिन्छ । रोग फैलाउने जीवाणु धेरै समयसम्म जीवीत रहने र माटोलाई बिगाड गर्ने क्षमता राख्छन् । नदीले काठमाडौं नछोडेसम्म त्यसको पानी शरीरसँगको सम्पर्कको लागि पनि योग्य छैन । गोकर्णसम्म नदीको पानी आशिंक रुपमा शरीरसँगको सम्पर्कको लागि पनि उपयुक्त छैन । चोभारसम्म नदीको पानी यस्तै रहेको छ । आशिंक सम्पर्कको अर्थ छोटो समयका लागि पानीमा शरीर भिजाउनु वा पानी छ्याप्नु हो । आँखाले हेर्दा खासै फोहोर नदेखिने ठाउँहरूमा हामीले बासिन्दाहरु यस पानीमा नुहाएको, लुगा धोएको र बालबालिकाहरु यस पानीमा वा ढल मिसिएको माटोमा खेलेको पायौं ।

उपत्यकाबाट बाहिर बग्ने ठाउँ चोभारमा जहाँ मनहरा र विष्णुमती नदीहरु मिसिन्छन्, ब्याक्टेरियाको मात्रा सबैभन्दा उच्च रहेको छ । यस स्थानमा ब्याक्टेरियाको संख्या खानलाई उपयुक्त हुने मात्राभन्दा १० लाख गुणा बढी, नुहाउनलाई उपयुक्त हुने मात्राभन्दा १०,००० गुणा बढी र केही क्षणको सम्पर्कका लागि उपयुक्त हुने मात्राभन्दा १००० गुणा बढी रहेको छ ।

Dr. Bidhuti Ranjan Jha regularly takes students and scientists to the headwaters of the Bagmati to document the native snow trout populations. Images courtesy Dr. Bidhuti Ranjan Jha.

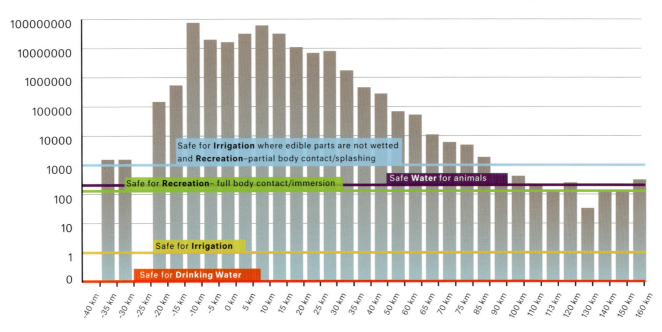

E. coli Colony counts
per 100ml (log10)

Safe for **Irrigation** where edible parts are not wetted and **Recreation**–partial body contact/splashing	
Safe for **Recreation**– full body contact/immersion	Safe **Water** for animals
Safe for **Irrigation**	
Safe for **Drinking Water**	

Sample sites (km from Chovar)

E. coli colony counts per 100ml of sample with Nepal water quality guidelines shown

The river's bacteria count is worse right before it leaves the valley at Chovar just downstream of where the Manohara and Bishnumati Rivers flow into the Bagmati. At this location, the bacteria count is a million times over the safe drinking levels, ten thousand times over the safe level for bathing and one thousand times over the safe level for briefly touching the water. Bacteria samples collected in the valley also indicated that over 90 percent of the samples were resistant to one form of antibiotic and over 45 percent were resistant to several drugs.

उपत्यकाबाट संकलन गरेका ब्याक्टेरियाका नमुनाबाट १० प्रतिशत ब्याक्टेरिया एक खालका एन्टिबायोटिक प्रतिरोधी पाइएका थिए भने ४५ प्रतिशत ब्याक्टेरिया एकमन्दा बढी एन्टिबायोटिक प्रतिरोधी रहेका थिए ।

Along with the toxicity levels of bacteria in the river, the expedition team also found high levels of chemicals from household and industrial waste. The data indicated unsafe levels of ammonia between -5km and 85km with especially high levels between -5km and 20km just downstream from some of the river's major tributaries. Chloride levels exceeded guidelines for irrigation between 0km and 20km where municipal waste dumping occurred along the river. Safe sodium levels for irrigation were also exceeded between 0km and 65km. These high levels could damage soil and future crop production. Unsafe iron levels were also high along the entire length of the river starting at -15km with the highest levels occurring at 20km. Manganese was also found to reach toxic levels from 0 km to 50 km.

हानीकारक ब्याक्टेरिया बाहेक नदीमा सोधकर्ताका समूहले उच्च मात्रामा घर तथा उद्योगबाट निस्किएका फोहोरमा रहेका रसायनहरु पनि पाएका थिए । तथ्याङ्क अनुसार ५ देखि ८५ किलोमिटरसम्म अमोनियाको उच्च मात्रा पाइएको थियो भने ५ किलोमिटरदेखि २० किलोमिटरसम्म यो मात्रा सबैभन्दा उच्च थियो । ० किलोमिटर देखि २० किलोमिटरसम्म जहाँ नगरपालीकाको फोहर फालिन्छ, नदीमा क्लोराइडको मात्रा उत्याधिक भएर पानी सिचाईको लागि अनुपयुक्त रहेको पाइयो । ० किलोमिटर देखि ६५ किलोमिटरसम्म सोडियमको मात्रा पनि सिचाईको लागि उपयुक्त मात्राभन्दा अधिक पाइयो । अत्याधिक मात्रामा रहेका यी रसायनहरुले माटोलाई हानी पुर्‍याउनुका साथै भविष्यमा बालीको उत्पादनमा पनि कमी ल्याउन सक्छन् । आइरनको मात्रा पनि पानीमा उच्च पाइयो जुन १५ किलोमिटरबाट सुरु भएर र २० किलोमिटरमा पुग्दा सबैभन्दा उच्च स्तरमा पुग्दछ । ० किलोमिटरदेखि ५० किलोमिटरसम्म पुग्दा म्याङ्गेनिजको मात्रा पनि उच्च पाइयो ।

Dr. Deep Narayan Shah, water quality specialist, provided a wealth of information about the Bagmati River during our interview at Kathmandu Contemporary Art Center in Patan.

The bacteria and chemical analysis of the river indicates that the entire length, apart from Baghdwar, is unsafe for drinking, human contact or irrigation. It is evident that more immediate attention needs to be taken in making the residents aware of health issues related to their interaction with the river. It is also clear that the most toxic levels of pollution occur at points in the river where it receives the sewage and industrial waste from the rest of the valley through its tributaries. The most hazardous accumulation occurs just as the river is forced through the rocky gorge at Chovar where the river flows black in color.

नदीको ब्याक्टेरिया र रसायनीक विश्लेषण अनुसार बाघद्वार बाहेक नदीको अन्य ठाउँको पानी खान, सिंचाई वा मानव सम्पर्क योग्य छैन । उपत्यकाका बासिन्दाहरुलाई पानीसँगको सम्पर्कले हुनसक्ने रोगबारे सतर्क बनाउनु अत्यन्त आवश्यक देखिन्छ । साथै आफ्ना सहायक नदीबाट ढल तथा कलकारखानाका फोहोर मिसिने ठाउँहरमा बागमती नदी सबैमन्दा प्रदुषित रहेको पाइयो । चोभारको ढुङ्गे घाटीको बिचबाट बग्ने बेलामा नदी सबैमन्दा प्रदुषित भई त्यसको पानी कालो देखिन्छ ।

As the Bagmati River leaves the Kathmandu Valley, it is squeezed through gorge at Chovar.

As part of this project, we are working with Sujan Chitrakar along with his colleagues and students at Kathmandu University to create public health brochures and posters in Nepalese that will outline the condition of the river and precautions to consider.

यस परियोजना अन्तर्गत, हामी सुजन चित्रकार तथा उनका सहकर्मी र काठमाडौँ विश्वविद्यालयका विद्यार्थीहरूसँग मिलेर नदीको अवस्था र काठमाडौँका बासिन्दाहरूले अपनाउनुपर्ने सतर्कता बारे नेपालीमा जनस्वास्थ्य सम्बन्धी पुस्तीकाहरु बनाउँदैछौँ ।

Sujan Chitrakar, head of Kathmandu University's Centre
for Art and Design and a socially conscience artist,
became an important contributor to the project.

This aerial photograph shows Kathmandu in 1967 with the Swayambhunath Temple as a bright round form on the left and the Tribhuvan International Airport on the right. This image was provided by the Amrit Bahadur Chitrakar Collection from the Nepal Picture Library.

The 2016 image from Google Earth Pro shows the urbanization in the valley over the past fifty years.

**Detailed View of Four Sites from the
Bagmati River Expedition**

For our project, we concentrated on four sites from the Bagmati River Expedition 2015 to present detailed documentation to provide a fuller understanding for our audience . The first site is upstream of the Sundarijil Dam
and picnic area which is indicated as the Expedition's 30 km sample site and where the bacteria from sewage
is evident in the water. It is downstream of the river's origins and upstream of where the Kathmandu Valley
gets most of its drinking water. To get to this site we drove 15 kilometres (9 mi) northeast from Kathmandu and
then walked three hours uphill from the market and bus stop. As we walked up the hill on partially constructed
steps, we saw a large pipe that brought water to the valley positioned next to the path. After seeing the small
dam and size of the pipeline, it was hard to believe that this system served 3 million residents. Along the path
on our right, were sewage lines leading to the river's edge. After we got to the park, we walked across the dam
and headed upstream to find the expedition's GPS coordinates. In the distance, we could see villages and farm-
land cut into the hillsides. While drawing and video taping the area around the site, a small herd of goats came
up to us. Before we left, we decided to taste the Bagmati. After running the water through our Grayl travel filter,
there was a sense of other-worldliness to drinking the holy water. I felt more connected to the river and that
feeling still remains. I imagine that that reaction is a very tiny reflection of how Hindus and Buddhists feel about
their connection to the Bagmati. To bathe in and drink its water connects them to past generations, to various
deities, and intangible spirituality that connects everything.

हाम्रो परियोजना अन्तर्गत हामीले बागमती नदी यात्रा २०१५ बाट चार स्थलहरु चयन गरी तिनीहरुको विस्तृत विवरण प्रस्तुत गर्न खोजेका छौं । पहिलो स्थल सुन्दरीजल बाँधभन्दा माथिको पिकनिक स्थल हो जसलाई यात्राको ३० औं नमूना स्थलको रुपमा इंगित गरिएको छ र जहाँ ढलबाट मिसिइएको ब्याक्टेरिया पाइएको थियो । यो स्थल नदीको मूलभन्दा तल र काठमाडौंमा आपूर्ती हुने खानेपानीको स्रोतभन्दा माथि हो । हामी गाडीमा १५ किलोमिटर र त्यसपछि बजार र बसपार्कबाट ३ घण्टा उकालो हिंडेर यस ठाउँमा पुग्यौं । उकालोमा बनेको भ्याड चढ्दै गर्दा हामीले बाटोको छेउमा काठमाडौंमा पानी पुर्‍याउने ठूलो पाइप देख्यौं । बाँध र पाइपको आकार हेर्दा यहाँबाट ३० लाख बासिन्दालाई खानेपानीको आपूर्ती हुन्छ भन्दा अचम्म मान्नुपर्ने अवस्था थियो । बाटोमा दायाँतिर नदीसम्म पुग्ने ढलको पाइप थियो । निकुञ्जमा पुगेपछि हामीले यात्राबाट प्राप्त जिपिएसको कोओर्डिनेट मेटाउन बाँध पारी गएर माथितिर उक्लियौं । हामीभन्दा पर डाँडामा रहेका गाउँ र खेतहरुको दृश्य देख्न सकिन्थ्यो । त्यस क्षेत्रको चित्र कोर्दा र फोटो खिच्दै गर्दा हामी सामू बाख्राको एक बथान आइपुग्यो । त्यहाँबाट हिंड्नु अगाडी हामीले बागमतीको पानी चाख्ने निर्णय गर्‍यौं । हामीले बोकेका फिल्टरबाट पानीलाई प्रशोधित गरे पश्चात उक्त पवित्र पानी खाँदा एक अलग संसारमा पुगेको अनुभव भयो । मैले बागमतीसँग आत्मीयता महसुस गरें र मभित्र त्यो अनुभूती अहिलेसम्म पनि जीवित नै छ । मलाइ लाग्दछ बागमतीसँग हिन्दु र बौद्ध धर्मावलम्बीहरुले अनुभव गर्ने गरेका सम्बन्धको त्यो एक सानो प्रतिबिंब थियो । यस नदीमा नुहाउँदा र यसको पानी खाँदा तीनीहरुले आफूलाई आफ्नो पूर्व जीवन, विभिन्न देवीदेवता र सबैलाई जोड्ने आध्यात्मसँग नजिक पाउँछन् ।

Alberto is holding his sketch on location at Shivapuri Nagarjun National Park.

Bagmati River Headwaters - 1:15 pm - March 16, 2016 - long walk up here - 5,283 ft - elevation

This is a detail of the sketch at Bagmati River Expedition sample site # ~30km which is upstream of the dam at Sundarijal in the Shivapuri Nagarjun National Park.

The water is crystal clear near the headwaters at Bagmati River Expedition sample site # -30km in Shivapuri Nagarjun National Park.

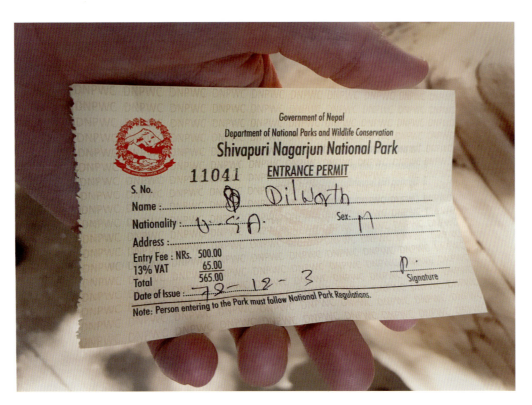

Jason is holding the entrance ticket to Shivapuri Nagarjun, National Park. After a long uphill trek to reach the park, we almost did not get permission to enter because we did not realize that we needed our passports for identification.

This oil paint line drawing of Bagmati River Expedition sample site # -30km in Shivapuri Nagarjun. National Park was created as a preliminary study for a painting.

This oil painting is of the Bagmati River Expedition sample site # - 30km in Shivapuri Nagarjun National Park.

Along the banks of the Bagmati River in Shivapuri Nagarjun, National Park is sand that cleanses the water. This sand is found throughout the river except in the most polluted parts in the valley where it has been heavily excavated.

Dr. David Gillete and Alberto taste the Bagmati River near the headwaters. They use a Grayl filter as a precaution against the unsafe bacteria count that is already present.

The second site is at Gokarnewor at 20 km sample site. It is just downstream of where the river flows through a pass leading into the Kathmandu Valley and is just outside the city of Kathmandu. We had passed this location on the way up to Sundarijil Dam the previous day. At the pass, there is a smaller dam that controls flow during the monsoon season. Below the dam was a series of exposed rocks and boulders that were used to dry the clothes that had been recently washed in the river. Downstream we could see several women rubbing garments against rocks in the river and along side them was a partially clothed middle-aged man bathing himself. Our site coordinates brought us another 100 meters downstream next to a long narrow flat strip of land that flanked the sides of the river. Several stones had been placed across the river in a row to allow the residents to cross the slow moving water. Just downstream, we could see a large cement waste water pipe pointing toward the river. Upstream were two boys walking in the middle of the river heading toward a women carry two buckets of water to pour over her neatly-arranged lines of crops. As I document the location, a young man in a motorcycle veered off the path to miss me and fell into the foot-deep river.

दोस्रो ठाउँ २० किलोमिटर नमूना स्थल, गोकर्णेश्वरमा रहेको छ । काठमाडौं शहरको ठीक बाहिर यसै ठाउँबाट बागमती उपत्यकाभित्र बग्ने गर्छ । हामी सुन्दरीजल जाँदा यही बाटोबाट गएका थियौं । वर्षा याममा नदीको बहाव नियन्त्रित गर्न यहाँ एक सानो बाँध बनाइएको छ । नदी किनारमा केही महिलाहरु ढुङ्गामाथि लुगा धोइरहेकी थिइन भने छेउमा एक अर्धनग्न अधबैंसे पुरुष नुहाइरहेका थिए । हामी १०० मिटर तल पुगेर नदी किनारमा रहेको साँघुरो समतल भागमा रहेको आफ्नो स्थलमा आइपुग्यौं । नदीमा आरपार गर्न कम बहाव भएको पानीमा सानासाना ढुङ्गाहरु राखिएका थिए । अलि तलतिर सिमेन्टले बनेको ढल नदीको दिशामा राखिएको थियो । अलि माथि बालीहरुमा पानी हाल्न दुई बालक नदीको बीचमा दुई वटा बाल्टिन लिएर एक महिलातिर जाँदै थिए । स्थलको अवलोकन गर्दैगर्दा मोटरसाइकलमा मतिर आउँदै गरेका एक युवक मलाई जोगाउन मोटरसाइकलसहित कुर्कुच्चासम्म आउने पानीमा लड्न पुगे ।

This video still captures a minor motorcycle accident on the Bagmati River at Gokarneswor while we were documenting the site.

This oil paint line drawing of the Bagmati River flood gates below Gokarna was created as a preliminary study for a painting.

This oil painting is of the Bagmati River flood gates below Gokarna on the outskirts of Kathmandu.

Two residents cross the shallow Bagmati River at Bagmati River
Expedition sample site #-20km in Gokarneswor.

This oil paint line drawing of the Bagmati River Expedition sample site # ~20km in Gokarneswor was created as a preliminary study for a painting

Looking downstream from the walking bridge at Gueswori Temple in Kathmandu, one can see the ancient temple on the left and new urban development on the right separated by the Bagmati River in the middle.

The third location is at Gueswori, marked as the 15 km site, which is near the heart of the city, It is perhaps the most sacred section of the river and includes the Pashupatinath and Gueswori Temples. The Pashupatinath Temple is the oldest temple in Kathmandu and an UNESCO Heritage Site. As I walked across the metal bridge over the Bagmati River heading toward the Gueswori Temple and our GPS coordinates, I looked downstream and saw cows grazing in the grasses growing in the river. It reminded me of many 19th century paintings of cows feeding along the Thames. I was surprised at how pastoral it appeared amidst the sounds of traffic, litter on the banks and the crowded Kathmandu neighborhood that bordered the river. Upstream I saw a bittersweet scene of a father and his daughter bathing together at the base of a stone embankment used for funeral pyres. The young girl was thoroughly enjoying herself as she dunked her head underwater to remove the suds from her hair. Just downstream about 15 yards on the edge of the river, a long orange piece of fabric from a recent funeral ritual slowly waved back and forth in the current. As I worked on my second drawing, one of the cows that I had seen earlier meandered next to me as a young timid monkey carefully walked around me. When I was finished with the drawing, I looked up and saw a couple of girls in their school uniforms building makeshift water balloons by filling their lunch's zip locked bags with river water and throwing them at their class-mates. As they ran down the street laughing, a young man with a simple white fabric wrapped around his waist slowly walked down to the river's edge and placed a large bowl-shaped leaf into the slow current. As it drifted closer to me, I could see ashes under a small bright yellow piece of cloth.

शहरको मुटुमा अवस्थित गुहेश्वरी, १५ किलोमिटर नमूना स्थल, हाम्रो अवलोकनको क्रममा तेस्रो ठाउँ थियो । पशुपतीनाथ र गुहेश्वरी मन्दिर रहेको यो ठाउँ शायद नदीको सबैभन्दा पवित्र मानिने स्थल हुनुका साथै युनेस्कोको अन्तर्गतको विश्व सम्पदा पनि हो । बागमती नदीमाथिको फलामे पुलबाट गुहेश्वरी तीर हिँड्दै गर्दा मैले तल गाईहरूले पानीमा उम्रिएका घाँस खाइरहेका देखें । यो दृश्य हेर्दा मलाई थेम्स नदीको किनारमा गाईहरू चर्दै गरेको दृश्य भएको १९ औं शताब्दीको एक पेन्टिङको सम्झना आयो । मलाई आश्चर्य भयो कि गाडीहरुको आवाज, नदी किनारमा रहेको फोहर र अलि पर नै भिडभाडले भरिएको काठमाँडौ शहरको बिच पनि त्यो ठाउँमा एक ग्रामीण वातावरणको बोध हुन्थ्यो । अलि माथि चिता जलाउन प्रयोग हुने ढुङ्गे तटबंधमा एक पिता र पुत्री नुहाँउदै गरेको सुन्दर तर मार्मिक दृश्य थियो । आफ्नो कपालबाट साबुन पखाल्न पानीमा डुब्की लगाँउदै गरेकी त्यो केटी रमाउँदै थिइन । अलि पर भर्खरै अन्तिम संस्कारको लागि प्रयोग गरिएको सुन्तला रङको कपडा पानीमा बगीरहेको थियो । मैले दोस्रो चित्र कोर्दै गर्दा अधि देखेको गाई मतिर आयो भने एउटा डराएको बाँदर मेरो वरिपरि सावधानीपूर्वक हिँडन थाल्यो । मैले चित्र कोरिसकेर माथि हेर्दा विद्यालयको लुगा लगाएकी दुई बालिकाले आफ्नो खाजाको झोलामा पानी भरेर पानीको बेलुन बनाई आफ्ना साथीहरुमाथि फाल्दै गरेको देखें । तिनिहरु हाँस्दै बाटोमा दगुर्दै गर्दा पहेँलो वस्त्रमा बेरिएका एक युवक नदीको किनारमा पुगी पातले बनेको ठूलो टपरी पानीमा बगाउँदै थिए । म नजिकै आइपुग्दा मैले त्यस टपरीमा खरानी र सुन्दर पहेँलो फूल देखें ।

Video still depicts a father and daughter bathing in front of a funeral pyre platform in the polluted Bagmati River at the Gueswori Temple, part of a sacred Hindu UNESCO Heritage Site.

Video still captures an offering of funeral pyre remains into the Bagmati River in Guheswori Temple.

This oil paint line drawing of Bagmati River Expedition sample site # ~15km by Guheswori Temple was created as a preliminary study for a painting

The oil painting is of the Bagmati River Expedition sample site # ~15km by Guheswori Temple.

Alberto draws on the bank of the Bagmati River in front of the 400 hundred- year-old Guheswori Temple.

1:36 pm - Guhesuri, Kathmandu, Nepal - March 18, 2016

Looking upstream at the Bagmati River, funeral pyres burn in front of the Pashupatinath Temple that is part of a sacred Hindu UNESCO Heritage Site, which, some believe, originated in 400 BC. On the right, are the 15 shrines of Pandra Shivalaya.

3:40 pm ~ March 19, 2016 ~ Pashupatinath, Kathmandu, Nepal

The last site is at Chovar, marked as 0 km, and is where the river exits the valley. It is one of the most polluted sections in the river. It is also the site of Adinath Lokeshwar Mandir Temple, which is sacred to both Hindus and Buddhists. The winding drive up to Chovar ends in a parking lot full of cars, motorcycles and buses. The walkway took us toward the temple and then toward the gorge that had been cut in the mountain. We had just come from Guheswori where the bacteria count was seven times over the safe level recommended for brief human contact and around seventy times higher than recommended for bathing, but the water was only slightly stained. This was due in part to the low volume of water and the sand in the river, which helped filter some of the waste. Just 15 km (9 miles) down-stream, however, the water was now running black and odorous. Bacteria levels had jumped from 7,000 to 100,000 colonies of bacteria per milliliter (0.2 teaspoon). At the bottom of the gorge, an eddy had formed where a piece of white Styrofoam was continuously circling slowly in the dark liquid. Next to the platform where I was standing was a small temple with a bell. Inside was a stone sculpture of a religious deity, but the facial features had been worn down by six hundred years of hands touching the head as part of Hindu and Buddhist pilgrimages. All that remained where the forehead would be, were traces of bright red pigment.

 Downhill of the gorge is the Adinath Lokeshwor Temple. Behind it was a long flat wide plain with a couple of cows and buffalo using their heads to rummage through the piles of litter. After sitting down to start my documentation, I had a small thin man stand beside me who watched me draw for 20 minutes. A couple of children joined him for a few minutes before they moved on to find something more interesting.

हाम्रो अन्तिम स्थल थियो ० किलोमिटर अंकित गरिएको चोमार जहाँबाट नदी काठमाडौँबाट बाहिर बग्दछ । नदीको सबैभन्दा प्रदुषित क्षेत्रमध्ये यो एक हो । यस स्थलमा हिन्दु र बौद्ध धर्मावलम्वी दुवैले मान्ने आदिनाथ लोकेश्वर मन्दिर पनि छ । चोमारसम्मको घुमावदार बाटो कार, बस र मोटरसाइकलहरुले भरिएको पार्किङ स्थलमा गएर अन्त्य हुन्छ । हामी हिँडेर मन्दिर र त्यसपछि पहाडमा बनेको घाटीमा पुग्यौं । हामी भर्खरै गुहेश्वरीबाट आएका थियौँ जहाँ ब्याक्टेरियाको संख्या क्षाणिक सम्पर्कको लागि योग्य हुने मात्रा भन्दा ७ गुणा बढी र नुहानलाई सुरक्षित हुने मात्राभन्दा ७० गुणा बढी थियो तर पानी अलिकती मात्र धमिलो थियो । पानीको कम मात्रा र फोहोर चाल्नी गर्ने बालुवाले गर्दा यस्तो भएको हुनुपर्छ । तर मात्र १५ किलोमिटर दुरीमा रहेको यो ठाउँमा पानी कालो र दुर्गन्धित थियो । ब्याक्टेरियाको संख्या पनि ७,००० बाट १००,००० कोलोनि प्रति मिलिलिटर पुगेको थियो । घाटीको तल्लो भागमा सेतो स्टायरोफोमको एक टुकडा पानीमा गोलोगोलो घुम्दै गरेको थियो । म उभिएको ठाउँको छेउमा एउटा घण्टी भएको मन्दिर थियो । मन्दिरभित्र देउताको एउटा मूर्ति थियो तर ६०० वर्षदेखि हिन्दु र बौद्ध श्रद्धालुले छुँदै आएकोले मूर्तीको अनुहार बिग्रिएर रातो रङ्ल पोतिएको निधार मात्र देखिन्थ्यो ।

धाटीबाट तलतिर आदिनाथ लोकेश्वर मन्दिर थियो । मन्दिरको पछाडीको समतल जमिनमा दुई वटा गाईहरु फोहोरको थुप्रोमा खानेकुरा खोज्दै थिए । चित्र कोर्न बस्दा एक जना दुब्लो पुरुष मेरो छेउमा आएर उभिए र २० मिनेटसम्म मैले चित्र कोरेको हेरिरहे । दुइ जना बालबालिका पनि केही क्षण पछि आए तर केहि मिनेट पछि अन्तै गए ।

Video still provides a close view of the Bagmati River
at the bottom of the gorge at Chovar.

On the banks of the Bagmati River in Chovar, one can see the Jal Binayak Temple, an important Hindu temple built in 1602.

This stage can be found inside the deserted Himal Cement Factory, which was built in 1974 and was the Kathmandu Valley's first cement factory. It was closed in 2002 after it was discovered that it produced half of the valley's air pollution.

3:20pm · Chobar ~ Bagmati Ruins · March 19, 2016

Sketch near the Bagmati River Expedition sample site # 0km at Chovar.

This oil paint line drawing looking upstream at Bagmati River Expedition sample site # 0km at Chovar was created as a preliminary study for a painting.

This oil painting is of the Jal Binayak Temple at the Bagmati River Expedition sample site #0km at Chovar.

The 1956 photograph looking across the Bagmati River at Jal Binayak Temple in Chovar showed the river at flood stage. This image was provide by the Mukunda Bahadur Shrestha Collection from the Nepal Picture Library.

The 1956 photograph looking downstream at the Bagmati River and the Jal Binayak Temple from on top of the gorge in Chovar shows the river at flood stage. This image was provided by the Mukunda Bahadur Shrestha Collection from the Nepal Picture Library.

This oil paint line drawing looking downstream at Bagmati River Expedition sample site #0km at Chovar was created as a preliminary study for a painting.

This oil painting is looking downstream from the Bagmati River Expedition sample site # 0km at Chovar.

These images depict the bathing ceremony of the Machhindranath at Chovar in the 1970's. This image was provided by the Mukunda Bahadur Shrestha from the Nepal Picture Library.

Jeff Davids, water specialist and president of H2Otech, created this drawing as he explained the number of complex issues that affect the groundwater in the Kathmandu Valley.

Water, Water, Everywhere, Nor Any Drop to Drink

"Water, water, everywhere, Nor any drop to drink."
The Rime of the Ancient Mariner, by Samuel Taylor Coleridge

Freshwater is the most important commodity in the world. Seventy-one percent of the earth's surface is covered by water but 97.5 % is saltwater. Of the remaining 2.5 %, which is freshwater; 69% is frozen in glaciers and ice caps, 30% is groundwater, and only 1% is surface water. Of that small percentage of surface water, most is ground ice and permafrost with lakes and rivers only accounting for 30.5 %. That means that less than one percent of all the world's water is easily accessible in freshwater rivers and lakes. Nepal's freshwater supply is ranked 41st out of 170 countries. It is rich in freshwater resources but 90% is only available during the four summer monsoon months while some of the other months regularly experience prolonged droughts. As one of the poorest and least developed countries in the world, Nepal cannot afford the infrastructure to build large reservoirs that could dispense its water and hydroelectricity throughout the year. Nepal energy consumption is surprisingly low and is only a third of the average for Asia and one-fifth the worldwide average. It provides only 43% of its residents with electricity, most of whom live in urban areas, and 76% of it residents depend on wood for cooking, which explains some of the deforestation that occurs. The lack of electricity not only affects the economy, but it also affects the ability of municipalities to pump groundwater, run water and sewage treatment plants and provide other services. The lack of infrastructure and coordinated services also means that the residents of Nepal and Kathmandu valley often are without water during the driest months of the year. This spring, the drought has been worse than normal because of the increased warming trends from climate change and the damage to water pipes caused by the recent earthquake.

"जता ततै छ पानी, छैन खानलाई एक बूँद पनि"

'जता ततै छ पानी, छैन खानलाई एक बूँद पनि"
स्याम्युल टेलर कोलरिजद्वारा लिखित कविताबाट

सफा खानेपानी सबैभन्दा महत्वपूर्ण वस्तु हो । पृथ्वीको ७१ प्रतिशत भाग पानी भएपनि १७.५ प्रतिशत पानी नुनिलो छ । बाँकी २.५ प्रतिशत सफा पानीको पनि ६९ प्रतिशत हिमनदीमा जमेको पानी हो, ३० प्रतिशत जमिनमुनी छ भने १ प्रतिशत मात्र सतही पानी हो । सतही पानीमध्ये पनि धेरैजसो हिउँको रुपमा रहेको छ भने मात्र ३०.५ प्रतिशत नदी र तालको रुपमा रहेको छ । यसको मतलब पृथ्वीमा भएको पानीमध्ये एक प्रतिशतभन्दा कम मात्र उपयोग गर्न सकिने रुपमा उपलब्ध छ । नेपालमा सफा पानीको आपूर्ती १७० देशमध्ये ४१ औं स्थानमा पर्छ । जलस्रोतको धनी देश भएपनि गर्मी र वर्षा यामको चार महीनामा मात्र १० प्रतिशत पानी उपलब्ध हुन्छ भने अरु महीना सुक्खा हुने गर्छन् । गरीब र अविकसित मुलुक भएकोले नेपालले वर्षभरी खानेपानी आपूर्ती र जलविद्युतका उत्पादन गर्नका लागि आवश्यक ठूलो जलाशयको निर्माण गर्नसकेको छैन । नेपालमा उर्जाको खपत आश्चर्यजनक रुपले कम छ र एशियामा औसत रुपले खपत हुने उर्जाको एक तिहाई र विश्वमा औसत रुपले खपत हुने उर्जाको एक्को पाचौं भाग रहेको छ । नेपालमा जनसंख्याको ४३ प्रतिशतलाई मात्र बिजुलीको सुविधा उपलब्ध छ जसमध्ये अधिकांश बासिन्दाहरु शहरमा बस्छन जबकी ७६% जनसंख्या खाना पकाउन दाउरामा निर्भर छ र यो वन फँडानीको मुख्य कारण पनि हो । बिजुलीको अभावले अर्थव्यवस्था मात्र कमजोर पार्ने होइन नगरपालिकाको जमिनमुनिबाट पानी तान्ने, आपूर्ती गर्ने, ढल व्यवस्थापन गर्ने र अन्य सेवा प्रदान गर्ने क्षमतामा पनि असर पार्दछ । पूर्वाधार र समन्वयित सेवाको कमीले गर्दा काठमाडौं र नेपालका बासिन्दाहरुलाई सुक्खा याममा पानीको अभाव हुने गर्छ । यसपल्टको बसन्त ऋतुमा मौसम परिवर्तनले गर्दा बढेको तापक्रम र भुकम्पले गर्दा खानेपानीको पाइपमा पुगेको क्षतिका कारण सुक्खाको समस्या अझ गम्भीर भएको छ ।

This page in Alberto's sketchbook includes the dust mask he used during his two- week trip to the Kathmandu Valley.

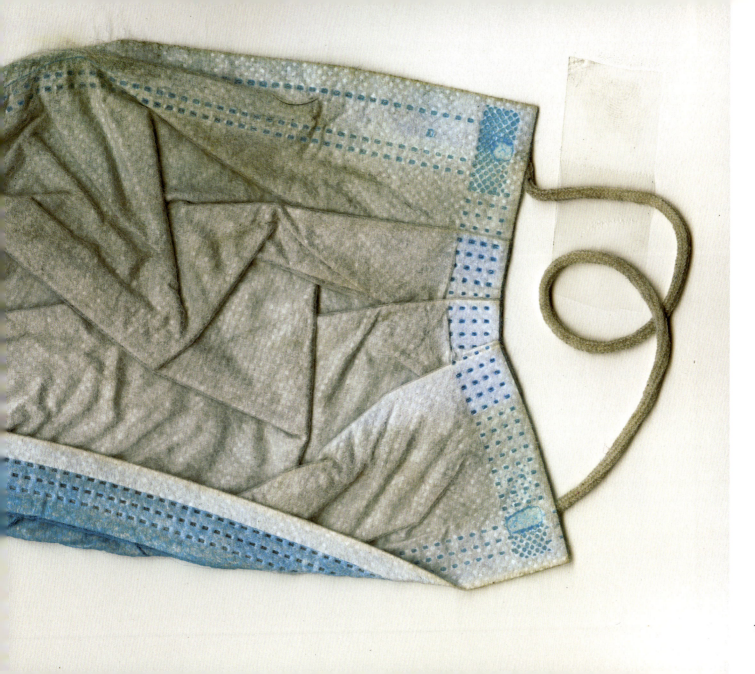

Nepal's ability to construct expensive infrastructure has been limited by its ability to attract foreign investors. The Asian Development Bank has been the cornerstone of most of the country's major improvement projects. China has recently also become Nepal's top foreign investor with a major hydroelectric project scheduled to be built in western Nepal. The Asia Development Bank is a financial institution established to promote economic growth and cooperation in the poorest countries in Asia. Nepal, however, continues to have the least foreign investment of any country in South Asia. Its economy relies heavily on agriculture and tourism. Lack of infrastructure and planning have affected the ability of both to grow to their full potential. The inconsistent availability of water and increase in pollution continues to be an issue for farmers especially those located downstream of Kathmandu Valley. Tourism, mostly from India, China and the United States, is negatively affected by the lack of clean water and air in Kathmandu Valley where many visitors have to don hospital masks to evade the toxic dust that causes the "Kathmandu cough". Reports show that most visitors make a quick stop in the valley before they move on to the national parks and other natural attractions. The city's cultural significance is being degraded by urban crowding and pollution. Before the mass migration into the city that started after 1950 and accelerated industrialization during the 1970's, sentries could be found along the sacred Bagmati River. These sentries protected the river from litter and activities that might degrade the sacred river. Now the river is only protected by regulations that are not being enforced, weekly clean-ups that bring communities together to address selected sections of the river's banks and a festival that brings awareness to the plight of the river, but there still remains very little that is done to clean this holy water.

नेपालको महँगो पूर्वाधार निर्माण गर्ने क्षमता यसको विदेशी लगानीकर्तालाई आकर्षित गर्न सक्ने क्षमताले निर्धारित गर्छ । नेपालको धेरैजसो प्रमुख विकास परियोजनाको मुख्य सहयोगी एशियन विकास बैंक रहेको छ । भर्खरै पश्चिम नेपालमा ठूलो जलविद्युत परियोजना बनाउने सम्झौतासँगै चीन पनि नेपालको सबैभन्दा ठूलो विदेशी लगानीकर्ता भएको छ । एशियाका गरीब मुलुकहरूको आर्थिक वृद्धि र तिनीहरूबिचको सम्बन्धलाई विस्तार गर्ने उद्देश्यले एशियन विकास बैंकको स्थापना गरिएको थियो । तथापि नेपालले दक्षिणी एशियाका अरु देशहरुको तुलनामा सबैभन्दा कम विदेशी लगानी प्राप्त गर्ने गरेको छ । नेपालको अर्थव्यवस्था कृषि र पर्यटनमा अत्याधिक निर्भर गर्दछ तर पूर्वाधार र योजनाको कमीले दुवै क्षेत्र पूर्ण रूपले विकसित हुनसकेका छैनन् । कृषकहरू र खासगरी काठमाडौं उपत्यकाभन्दा तलतिरका कृषकहरु पानीको अपर्याप्त आपूर्ती र बढ्दै गएको प्रदुषणले समस्याग्रस्त छन् । भारत, चिन र अमेरिकाबाट आउने पर्यटकको संख्या सफा खाने पानी र स्वच्छ हावाको अभावले घट्दै गरेको छ । धेरैजसो पर्यटकले यहाँको प्रदुषित पानी र खासगरी हावाबाट हुने काठमाडौं खोकी बाट बच्न मास्क लगाएर हिँड्ने गर्छन् । तथ्याङ्क अनुसार धेरैजसो पर्यटकहरु काठमाडौंमा छोटो समय मात्र बसेर राष्ट्रिय निकुञ्ज र अन्य पर्यटकिय स्थलतिर लाग्ने गरेका छन् । उपत्यकाको सांस्कृतिक महत्व यहाँको मीडभाड र प्रदुषणले घट्दै गएको छ । १९५० तिरको जन प्रवास र १९७० तिरको तीव्र औद्योगीकरण पूर्व बाग्ममती नदीको किनारमा सिपाहीहरू देख्न सकिन्थे । सिपाहीहरूले नदीलाई फोहोर हुनबाट जोगाउने काम गर्थे । अहिले नदीको सुरक्षा लागू हुननसकेका नियमावली, नदीका केही भाग सफा गर्न एकजुट भई साप्ताहिक रुपमा लाग्ने समुदायहरु र नदीको बेथिति बारे सतर्क बनाउने पर्वले गर्ने गरेका छन् तर यी सबैको उपलब्धी न्यून रहेको छ ।

The availability of clean water continues to be a major health issue in the Valley. Over 70 percent of the residents are connected to the city's water, but 94% of the drinking water contains unsafe levels of bacteria. Chlorine levels in the city's water are often too low to be effective and due to the amount of leakage from water and sewage lines, water is often contaminated as soon as it leaves the water treatment plants. There are times during the dry seasons, when the city cannot supply water to all of its residents. The Nepalese are then forced to rely on one of 700 privately-owned water tankers of which only 400 are officially registered or one of the 600 water bottling companies of which half are officially certified. Both options are much more costly than the city's water supply, but the alternative certified water suppliers can provide much safer water. Their water usually comes from aquifers in the city's outskirts, but since there are few extraction regulations, these communities are being affected by the constant water removals. The other option to access water is by tapping into the valley's groundwater. Although almost half of the city's water comes from the groundwater in the wet season and 70 percent during the dry season, that supply has also become contaminated by sewage and industrial waste from leaking pipes. There are also an additional 2000 unregulated boreholes tapping into the Valley's groundwater by households, factories and hotels. Thirty percent of the population in the valley depends on the groundwater, but 80 % of the water is microbiologically unsafe. The April earthquake has also created havoc to the groundwater supply lines. Ten of the city's 70 wells have become disconnected and supplies have dropped by 7 million liters per day (almost 2 million gallons) compared from this same period last year. Countless other private wells have also become disconnected from the groundwater supplies. Groundwater, however, continues to be extracted at a rate that is six times higher than its ability to recharge.

सफा पानीको आपूर्ती अहिले पनि उपत्यकाको स्वास्थ्य सम्बन्धी सबैभन्दा ठूलो मुद्दा रहेको छ । ७० प्रतिशतभन्दा बढी बासिन्दाहरुलाई पानीको आपूर्ती गरिएपनि १४% पानीमा ब्याक्टेरियाको संख्या सुरक्षित स्तरभन्दा माथि छ । पानीमा क्लोरिनको मात्रा आवश्यकभन्दा धेरै कम रहेको छ भने ढलबाट हुने चुहावटले गर्दा प्रशोधन केन्द्रबाट छोडिएको केही क्षणमै पानी प्रदुषित हुने गरेको छ । सुक्खा याममा शहरका सबै बासिन्दाहरुलाई पानी आपूर्ती गर्न सकिँदैन । यस्तो समयमा यहाँका बासिन्दाहरु ७०० वटा निजी कम्पनीद्वारा सञ्चालित पानीका ट्याङकर, जसमध्ये मात्र ४०० वटा कम्पनी आधिकारिक रुपमा दर्ता गरिएका छन्, वा ६०० वटा बोतलको खानेपानी कम्पनीहरु, जसमध्ये मात्र आधीजति आधिकारिक रुपमा प्रमाणित छन्, माथि निर्भर गर्नुपर्छ । दुवै विकल्प खानेपानी संस्थाबाट वितरण हुने पानीभन्दा महँगो पर्नजान्छन् तर तुलनात्मक रुपमा बढी सुरक्षित हुन्छन् । बोतल र ट्याङकर दुवैको पानी शहरको सिमानामा रहेका ढुङ्गाबाट प्राकृतिक रुपमा निस्किने पानीको स्रोतबाट आउँछ तर निरंतर पानी संकलनको क्रमले यहाँको समुदायलाई पनि असर गर्न थालेको छ । अर्को विकल्प उपत्यकाको जमिनमुनीको पानी हो । वर्षा याममा आधि र सुक्खा याममा ७० प्रतिशत पानी जमिनमुनीबाट आउने भएपनि ढल र चुहिने पाइपबाट निस्किने औद्योगिक फोहोरले गर्दा यो स्रोत पनि प्रदुषित हुनथालेको छ । कलकारखाना, घर र होटेलहरुले अनियंत्रित रुपमा २००० ठाउँमा जमिनमुनिको पानी निकाल्ने गरेका छन् । उपत्यकाको ३० प्रतिशत बासिन्दा जमिनमुनिको पानीमा निर्भर छन् तर ८० प्रतिशत पानि जिवाणुले खाने योग्य छैन । भुकम्पले सतही पानीको आपूर्तलाई पनि तहसनहस पारेको छ । शहरका ७० मध्ये १० वटा इनारहरु स्रोतसँग जोडिएका छैनन् भने अधिलो वर्ष यही समयको तुलनामा पानीको आपूर्तीमा ७० लाख लिटर प्रति दिनले कमी आएको छ । थुप्रै अरु इनारहरु पनि जमिनमुनीको पानीको स्रोतबाट अलग्गिएका छन् । तथापि जमिनमुनीको पानीको पुन: भरिने क्षमता भन्दा ६ गुणा बढी गतिमा पानी निकालिने क्रम जारी नै छ ।

The high rate of urban migration has been named as the major cause for most of the water issues and pollution in the valley, but when urbanization is planned and controlled, it can provide economic development and increased services. If it is not managed, as is the case in Kathmandu Valley, then industries are developed next to residential areas, buildings are built out of code and fail during earthquakes, vehicle emissions can grow to unsafe levels and services like sewage disposal and water delivery can become dysfunctional. Kathmandu Valley's lack of planning has created a situation where its air and water pollution are at extremely unsafe levels. The total length of all the cars (almost a million) surpasses the total length of roads and the unchecked emissions of these vehicles have contributed to major bronchial diseases in the cities. The valley's water continues to be affected by the daily disposal of 21,000 kg (23 tons) of untreated domestic sewage and over 3000 kg (over 3 tons) of untreated industrial waste into the Bagmati. The water is also negatively affected by the over 300 tons of solid waste that is dumped on its banks daily. The majority of the wastewater comes from the nearly half a million households in the valley that dispose of 75% of their consumed water into the river and tributaries. Consequently, studies have found that the river water volume increases everyday between 8-11am when most residents use their toilets. The 2,174 water-polluting industries in the valley also deposit toxic chemicals that contribute to the high levels of intestinal and skin diseases.

शहरी प्रवासको उच्च दरलाई नै पानीको अभाव र प्रदुषणको मुख्य कारणको रुपमा लिइने गरेको छ । नियोजित र नियन्त्रित रुपमा शहरी विकास गर्नसके आर्थिक विकास र सुलभ सेवा प्रदान गर्न सहज हुनसक्छ । तर यस्तो गर्न नसक्दा काठमाडौंमा जस्तै बस्ती नजिकै कारखाना निर्माण हुने, नियम विपरित घरहरु बन्ने र भुकम्पमा ढल्ने, गाडीहरुबाट खतरनाक मात्रामा धुँवा फालिने, ढल तथा पानी आपूर्ती अव्यवस्थित हुने जस्ता समस्याहरु हुनसक्छन् । उपत्यकाको अनियोजित विकासले गर्दा यहाँ पानी र हावाको प्रदुषण अत्याधिक स्तरमा पुगेको छ । उपत्यकामा रहेका सबै गाडीहरु (दस लाखभन्दा धेरै) को लम्बाई सडकको लम्बाइभन्दा अधिक छ र यी गाडीहरुबाट निस्किने धुवाँ फोक्सोका रोगहरुको मुख्य कारण हो । बागमतीमा दैनिक घरबाट फालिने २१००० किलो र कलकारखानाबाट फालिने ३००० किलो फोहोरले यहाँको पानीमा नराम्रो असर पुर्याउँदै आएको छ । नदी किनारमा फालिने दैनिक ६००,००० टन फोहोरले पनि बागमतीको पानीलाई प्रदुषित गर्दै आएको छ । प्रायजसो फोहोर पानी उपत्यका लगभग ५ लाख घरहरुबाट आउँछ जहाँबाट ७५ प्रतिशत फोहोर पानी बागमती र यसका सहायक नदीमा बगाइने गरिन्छ । अध्ययन अनुसार बिहान ८ बजेदेखि ११ बजेसम्म जब धेरैजसो बासिन्दाले शौचालयको प्रयोग गर्छन् नदीको पानीको स्तर बढ्ने गरेको छ । उपत्यकाका २१७४ उद्योगहरुले पनि विषादीयुक्त रसायन नदीमै फाल्ने गरेका छन् जसले गर्दा आँद्राको रोग तथा चर्म रोग हुने गरेको छ ।

The public bathroom at the market in Sundarijial before the entrance to Shivapuri Nagarjun National Park has its sewage line flowing directly into the Bagmati River.

Steep deforested hillsides along the Bagmati River create sedimentation and landslides.

To compound the issue of water scarcity and pollution in the valley, climate change has become an important factor in intensifying the need to take immediate action. The valley has been experiencing longer periods of drought, warmer temperatures and more intense periods of precipitation. The droughts and warmer temperatures reduce soil moisture, shorten the growing season, result in less food, decrease groundwater levels, reduce recharge abilities, decrease snowfall, reduce river flow, lessen hydroelectricity, increase water consumption (19 liters/5 gallons per day per person) and create more conflicts. The increased intense rainfall has created more flooding and landslides. The flooding has created damage to infrastructure, homes and crops and spread pathogens from the river and tributaries to the streets, yards, playgrounds, crops and soil. Landslides that have occurred along the steep hillsides in the upper Bagmati have also affected the infrastructure in the area. The flood of July 1993 deposited, in three days, seven times the annual average amount of sediment.

जलवायु परिवर्तनले पानीको अभाव र प्रदुषणको समस्या अझ जटिल पारेको छ । उपत्यकामा लामो समयसम्म सुक्खा हुने, तापक्रम बढ्दै गएको र धेरै पानी पर्ने समस्या देखिदै आएको छ । उच्च तापक्रम र सुक्खा यामले माटोको चिस्यानमा कमी आउने, बाली उम्रिने मौसम छोटो हुने, खाद्यान्नको उपजमा कमी आउने, नदीमा पानीको बहावमा कमी आउने, जलविद्युतमा कमी आउने, पानीको खपत बढेर जाने (१९ लिटर प्रति दिन प्रति व्यक्ति) र अझ धेरै द्वन्द्व सृजना हुने जस्ता समस्या हुने गरेका छन् । बढ्दै गएको वर्षाले बाढी र पहिरो पनि बढ्दै गएको छ । बाढीले पूर्वाधार, घरहरू र बाली नष्ट हुनुका साथै नदीमा रहेका जीवाणुहरू सडक, घरआँगन, खेल मैदान, बाली र माटोमा फैलिने गर्छन् । माथिल्लो बागमतीको डाँडामा जाने गरेको पहिरोले पनि पूर्वाधारमा असर पुर्‍याउँदै आएको छ । १९९३ को जुलाईमा आएको बाढीले वार्षिक औसत तलछटभन्दा सात गुणा बढी तलछट जम्मा गरेको थियो ।

The remains of one of the many great meals in Kathmandu Valley.

1:55 pm - 2:45 - with lunch in between drawing - Patan Museum - KCAC -
had a meeting today where we recorded some beautiful songs &
discussed residency plans with Sangeeta - March 14, 2016

Ink wash depicts one the many cluttered telephone poles in Kathmandu.

Moving forward

As was mentioned before, there is no shortage of documentation outlining recommendations on how to improve the condition in the Valley. What seems to be consistent amongst many of the reports is the need to use a multi-faceted approach for each issue and to empower communities to resolve some of the factors that are under their control. While the government has its hands full building new reservoirs and sewage treatment plants, laying many kilometers of new water pipes, and coordinating the new hydroelectric project, they are still unwilling to delegate responsibilities to communities and give up control of programs related to the river. There still remains a dire need for the government to enforce environmental regulations, provide urban planning, enforce building codes, start new wetland waste water treatment plants, provide maintenance of the prior water treatment plants, regularly test the water coming out of water treatment plants and manage vehicles emissions.

भविष्यतिर हेर्दा

हामीले पहिले पनि भनेका छौँ उपत्यकामा स्थितिलाई सुधार्न दिइएका सुझावहरुको दस्तावेजहरुको कमी छैन । धेरैजसो प्रतिवेदनहरुमा हरेक समस्याको समाधानका लागि बहुमुखी शैली अपनाउने र समुदायहरु अन्तर्गत पर्ने केही समस्याहरुको समाधान हेतु त्यहाँका बासिन्दाहरुलाई सक्षम बनाउने कुरा उल्लेख छ । नयाँ जलाशय र ढलको निर्माण, पाइपलाइन ओछ्याउने र नयाँ जलविद्युत परियोजनाको निर्माणलाई समन्वय गर्ने जस्ता काममा व्यस्त भएपनि सरकार नदी सम्बन्धित कार्य आफ्नो हातबाट समुदायहरुलाई हस्तान्तरण गर्न इच्छुक देखिदैन । सरकारले वातावरण सम्बन्धी ऐन लागू गर्ने, शहरी विकासको योजना बनाउने, भवन निर्माण सम्बन्धी कानून लागू गर्ने, फोहोर पानीको प्रशोधनका लागि नयाँ केन्द्र स्थापना गर्ने र पुरानोको रखरखाव गर्ने, पानी प्रशोधन केन्द्रबाट निस्किने पानीको नियमित जाँच गर्ने र गाडीबाट निस्किने धुवाँ नियन्त्रित गर्ने जस्ता काम तुरुन्त गर्नुपर्ने अत्यन्त आवश्यक छ ।

Near the Golden Temple in Patan, a home utilizes a water collection unit.

As is the case with any new democracy, there will continue to be more instability in the future, so it is imperative to use a bottom-up approach to resolve some of the most important health issues. Due to the significant levels of greenhouse gasses already in the atmosphere, and, since the majority of the illness causing waste comes from households, it is critical to continue with and begin new adaptive practices that will prepare the residents of the Valley to face these issues and plan for other challenges in the future. These plans should include starting educational awareness programs and policies that will promote point-of-use water purification procedures in homes, better hygiene practices, recycling of gray water for use in bathrooms and toilets, recycling waste which is up to 75% biodegradable, implementing rooftop rainwater harvesting, integrating more dry toilets, using more septic tanks that are not discharged into the rivers or tributaries and creating more public toilets for temporary squatters settlements. All of these efforts need to be carefully articulated by the municipalities, supported by the government and slowly implemented as part of a program to improve health conditions in the Valley. Collaboration is extremely important especially with the limited funds that are available. Collaboration exists during public awareness campaigns and symbolic events but is lacking in long term complex planning and implementation.

नयाँ लोकतन्त्रमा जहिले पनि केही समय अस्थिरताको वातावरण रहने हुँदा मुलभूत समस्याबाट सुरु गर्दै गम्भीर समस्याको समाधानतिर बढ्ने शैली अपनाउँदै सबैभन्दा पहिले अत्यन्त जरुरी स्वास्थ्य समस्याको समाधान गर्नु अझ आवश्यक देखिन्छ । किनकी सबैभन्दा बढी फोहोर पानी घरहरुबाट निस्किने गर्छ, मानिसहरुको प्रदुषित पानीसँगको संसर्ग निम्न पार्ने योजनामा समुदायले साथ दिनुपर्ने अझ आवश्यक देखिन्छ । साथै व्यक्तिगत र सामुदायिक रुपमा ने आधारभूत समस्याको समाधानका लागि नागरिकसँग उपलब्ध समाधानहरु सबैलाई उपलब्ध गराउनु पनि जरुरी छ । योजना अन्तर्गत घरमा पानी प्रशोधित गर्ने तरीका बारे जानकारीमूलक कार्यक्रम चलाउने, अझ स्वच्छ जीवनशैली, शौचालय र स्नानघरमा धमीलो पानीलाई प्रशोधित गर्ने प्रक्रया, ७५ प्रतिशतसम्म कुहिने फोहोरलाई फेरि प्रयोग गर्नसक्ने प्रक्रया, आकाशे पानी संकलन गर्ने, सुक्खा शौचालयको प्रयोग, सेप्टिक ट्याङ्कको प्रयोग, सुकुम्बासी बस्तीहरुमा सार्वजनिक शौचालय बनाउने जस्ता कार्यहरु हुनसक्छन । उपत्यकामा स्वास्थय सुधार योजना अन्तर्गत यी सबै कार्यक्रम सरकारको सहयोगमा नगरपालीकाले कार्यन्वयन गर्नुपर्छ । सीमित पूंजी भएको खंडमा आपसी सहयोग अनिवार्य देखिन्छ । जागरुकता अभियान र प्रतीकात्मक कार्यक्रममा सहकार्य देखिएपनि दीर्घकालीन योजना र कार्यन्वयनमा यसको कमी देखिन्छ ।

While there are over 100 organizations that have been formed over the past few decades to improve the Bagmati River and the Kathmandu Valley, their efforts could be more productive if collaboration occurred to take advantage of the limited funds that are available. There are, however, several community programs that have been very effective. Smart Paani is a private company established in 2011 that works with households, institutions and schools to introduce effective methods of rainwater harvesting, water filtration and water recycling. Another effective nongovernment organization is ENPHO, which was established in 1990. This organization provides training and works with communities to introduce locally-managed wetlands as a cost-effective approach to waster water treatment. They also work to integrate rainwater harvesting, ECOSAN toilets (waterless toilets) and water purification systems in households that use chlorine solution, SODIS (using sunlight to kill germs) and filters.

विगत केही दशकमा बागमती र काठमाडौँ उपत्यकामा परिवर्तन ल्याउन १०० मन्दा बढी संस्थाहरु गठन भएपनि तीनीहरुबिच सहकार्य गर्नसके सीमित पूंजीबाट उच्च लाभ लिन सकिन्थ्यो । तथापि केही सामुदायिक कार्यक्रमहरु धेरै प्रभावकारी पनि रहेका छन् । २०११ मा दर्ता गरिएको निजि कम्पनी स्मार्ट पानीले विभिन्न घर तथा संगठन र विद्यालयहरुसँग मिलेर आकाशे पानी संकलन, पानी प्रशोधन र पानीको पुन: प्रयोग सम्बन्धी विधिहरुबारे जानकारीमुलक कार्यक्रम चलाइरहेका छन् । १९९० मा दर्ता भएको इएनपिएचओ अर्को प्रभावकारी गैर सरकारी संस्था हो । यस संस्थाले फोहोर पानी प्रशोधनको लागि स्थानिय रुपले व्यवस्थापन गर्न सकिने सिमसार निर्माण गर्ने काम गर्दैछ । यसका साथै यस संस्थाले आकाशे पानी संकलन, बिना पानी सञ्चालन गर्न सकिने शौचालय, सोडिस, फिल्टर र क्लोरिनबाट पानी प्रशोधन गर्ने विधि पनि सञ्चालन गर्ने काम गर्छ ।

In front of the Shakya House, where we stayed in Patan, empty spaces had been converted into neighborhood gardens.

This ink wash is of an elderly woman who worked in Patan Durbar Square.

Patan Durbar
Square
March 2011

In 1993, Lumanti was formed to address the needs of the urban poor and those in temporary settlements along the river and elsewhere. Temporary squatters settlements continue to grow as increased migration raises prices for homes and forces relocation of the poor. The organization works to improve access to sanitation and clean water while improving settlements. They often work with community women's organizations to achieve their goals. Women are often burdened with the stress of finding clean water for their households. One of these well known women's organizations is the Women's Environment Preservation Committee (WEPCO). It empowers women and communities to become proactive in environmental issues and improving their neighborhood and households by incorporating community and home composting, paper collection, recycling and bio-gas production from organic (vegetable) waste.

शहरी गरीबहरु र सुकुम्बासीहरुको समस्या सम्बोधन गर्न सन् १९९३ मा लुमन्तीको गठन भएको थियो । शहरी प्रवाससँगै घरको मूल्य बढेर गरीबहरु विस्थापित हुँदै जाँदा सुकुम्बासीको संख्या बढ्दै गएको छ । लुमन्ती सुकुम्बासी बस्तीका बासिन्दाहरुलाई स्वच्छ जीवन र सफा पानी उपलब्ध गराउने काम गर्छ । यो संस्था प्राय सामुदायिक महिला समूहसँग मिलेर काम गर्छ । घरको लागि सफा पानी खोज्ने जिम्मेवारी प्राय महिलाले नै बेहोर्नुपरेको हुन्छ । महिला वातावरण संरक्षण समिति (वुमेन्स इनभारोमेन्ट प्रिजरभेसन कमिटी) यस्तै एक चित परिचित संगठन हो । यो संस्थाले महिलाहरु तथा समुदायलाई सशक्त बनाई वातावरण र आफ्नो टोललाई सुधार्न सामुदायीक तथा घरेलु स्तरमा फोहोरबाट मल बनाउने, कागज संकलन गर्ने, र कुहिने फोहोरबाट बायो ग्यास उत्पादन गर्ने जस्ता कार्यलाई प्रोत्साहन गर्छ ।

An 1853 watercolor by H.A. Oldfield from the Patan Museum depicts a pastoral scene on the Bagmati River with the Pashupatinath Temple in the background.

A good example of the government working with communities is seen in the Bagmati Mega Clean-up Campaign where government officials, security officers, members of the Nepali army and police, and members from over 950 organizations have come together on Saturday mornings since May of 2013 to clean the banks of the Bagmati River from Sundarijal to Chovar. Every week a specific section of the river is addressed. Since its inception, close to half a million people have participated and over 7,000 metric tons of solid waste have been removed from the banks of the river.

सरकार र समुदायको समन्वयको एउटा उत्तम उदाहरणको रुपमा बागमती सरसफाई अभियानलाई लिन सकिन्छ जसमा सरकारी कर्मचारी, सुरक्षा बल, नेपाल सेना र प्रहरीका जवान र १५० भन्दा बढी संघसस्थाका सदस्यहरु सहभागी भई मइ २०१३ देखि हरेक शनीबार बागमतीका किनारमा जम्मा भई सुन्दरीजलदेखि चोभारसम्मको सफाई गरेका थिए । हरेक हप्ता नदीको एक भागलाई सफा गरिन्छ । यस अभियानको सुरुवातदेखि लगभग ५ लाख मान्छे सहभागी भई ७,००० टनभन्दा बढी फोहोर नदीबाट निकालीसकेका छन् ।

Another noteworthy community organization and project that began in 2001 is the Bagmati River Festival, organized by the Nepal River Conservation Trust, which was started by a group of concerned river guides. The two and half month long festival incorporates the participation of 400 organizations, includes a river clean-up, tree planting, workshops, arts, music, poetry, literature, and water sports. It is one of the few conservation projects in the world that gives equal time to science, sports, conservation education, recreation, music, religion and social activities.

सन् २००१ मा सुरु भएको सामुदायिक संस्थाद्वारा सञ्चालित अर्को उल्लेखनीय परियोजना हो बागमती नदी महोत्सव । यो महोत्सव नदीका केही जागरुक गाइडहरुद्वारा चलाइएको नेपाल रिभर कन्जरभेसन ट्रस्ट (नेपाल नदी संरक्षण गुठी) द्वारा सञ्चालन गरिएको हो । ४०० संस्थाको सहभागिता रहेको दुई महीना लामो यस महोत्सवमा नदीको सफाई, वृक्षारोपण, कार्यशाला, कला, संगित, कविता, साहित्य र पानीमा खेलिने खेलहरु हुने गरेका छन् । यो परियोजना संसारका केही मात्र संरक्षण परियोजनाहरुभित्र पर्दछ जसमा विज्ञान, खेल, संरक्षण, शिक्षा, मनोरञ्जन, संगित, धर्म र समाजिक क्रियाकलापहरु समाविष्ट गरिने गरिन्छ ।

Inside our studio at the Kathmandu Contemporary Art Center, Pujan Gandharba and Amrit Gandhari performed the Bagmati River song we commissioned for the project's documentary.

This ink wash portrays one of the many unique commercial vehicles found in Kathmandu in the dust and the fading light of the evening.

Kathmandu, Nepal   March 2016

A great deal of good work is being done in the Kathmandu Valley at the grassroots level and the key to getting the most out of the limited manpower and funding is to collaborate on projects that can bring meaningful change to the residents of the valley. A little government support can sustain the work done to improve the basic needs of the residents of region.

उपत्यकामा समुदायिक स्तरमा धेरै कार्यहरू भइरहेका छन् र सीमित जनशक्ति र पूंजीबाट अधिक लाभ लिन र यहाँका बासिन्दाका जीवनमा अर्थपूर्ण बदलाव ल्याउन सहकार्य गर्न जरुरी छ । सरकारको सानो सहयोगले पनि यस क्षेत्रका बासिन्दाको जीवनमा बदलाव ल्याउन गरिएका कामलाई ठूलो टेवा पुग्नसक्छ ।

On our way back from Shivapuri Nagarjun National Park just outside the market in Sundarijil, we came across a pile of discarded bricks from the recent earthquake. The bricks seemed to symbolize a great deal about the country's struggles.

Communities around the world can draw inspiration from communities mentioned above in Kathmandu Valley. While this bottom-up approach is important in implementing safe practices at home and stemming other practices that contribute to the degradation of the environment that creates health hazards, governments need to provide the infrastructure to address the bigger issues of sewage and water treatment, urban planning, garbage disposal and enforcement of environmental regulations. There are many rivers around the world, including the Rhine River in Europe, the Cheonggyecheon River in South Korea and the Nanjing Qinhuai River in China, that had similar problems to the Bagmati River, and they have been restored.

विश्वभरका समुदायहरूले माथि उल्लिखित नेपालका समुदायबाट प्रेरणा लिन सक्छन् । निम्न तहदेखि सुरु गरेर माथिल्लो तहसम्म काम गर्ने निति घरमा सुरक्षित वातावरण बनाउने र स्वास्थ्यलाई हानी पुर्‍याउने कार्यहरूलाई निरुत्साहित गर्ने काम गरेपनि ढल, खानेपानी, शहरी विकास, फोहोर व्यवस्थापन र वातावरण सम्बन्धी नियमावली लागू गर्ने जस्ता कामका लागि चाहिने पूर्वाधार सरकारले उपलब्ध गराउन जरुरी छ । विश्वमा यस्तै अरु नदीहरु ज्स्तै युरोपको राइन नदी, दक्षिणी कोरियाको छियोङ्ग्येचोन नदी र चीनको नानजिङ किनहाई नदीमा पनि यस्तै समस्या थिए तर अहिले यी नदीहरुको सफाइ भइसकेको छ ।

On our walk into Patan, we encountered this rat along the path.

Patan, Nepal
March 2016

Although, it is always an ongoing battle of monitoring and enforcing regulations. One example mentioned, the Rhine River, faced more complicated issues. The Rhine's pollution started in the 1850's. It is over twice as long as the Bagmati and flows through six countries, although its tributaries are found in nine countries. At one point it was called the "Sewer of Europe", but in 1986, after a major chemical leak, the restoration efforts began. Twenty years and between 25-37 billion dollars later, the salmon are leaping again in the river. Sixty to seventy percent of the funds were spent on building wastewater treatment plants. The Rhine River's demise sounds very familiar, but its success was directly the result of international collaboration between the governments and nongovernment organizations who worked in the communities.

हुन त नियम तथा कानून लागू गर्नु निरन्तर चलिरहने संघर्ष हो । माथि दिइएका उदाहरणमध्ये राइन नदीमा धेरै समस्याहरु थिए । राइन नदी सन् १८५० देखि प्रदुषित हुन थालेको थियो । यो नदी बागमतीभन्दा दुई गुणा लामो छ र ६ वटा देशहरुमा बग्छ जबकी यसका सहायक नदीहरु ९ वटा देशहरुमा छन् । कुनै बेला यसलाई युरोपको ढल भनिने गरिन्थ्यो तर सन् १९८६ मा नदीमा रसायन चुहिँदा सरसफाई अभियानको सुरुवात भयो । २३ वर्ष र २५३७ अर्ब डलर पश्चात नदीमा फेरि पनि माछाहरु देखिन सकिन्छ । ६० देखि ७० प्रतिशत पूंजी फोहोर पानीको प्रशोधनमा खर्च भएको थियो । राइन नदीको विगती सुन्दा परिचित लाग्छ तर यसको सफलता सरकार र सामुदायिक स्तरमा कार्यरत गैर सरकारी संस्थाबिचको अन्तर्राष्ट्रिय समन्वयको नतिजा हो । बागमती नदीको प्रदुषण १०० वर्षभन्दा कम समयको नतिजा हो, यसको लम्बाई धेरै सानो छ र यो मात्र दुई देशको अधिनमा छ । यदी नेपाल सरकारले आफ्नो प्रयास बागमती नदी बग्ने एक उपत्यकामा मात्र केन्द्रित गर्ने हो भने पनि छोटो समयमा नै

High on top of a mountain on the edge of the Kathmandu Valley, hawks effortlessly glide on the currents above Swayambhunath. The 1500-year-old sacred Buddhist temple and UNESCO World Heritage Site is also known as the Monkey Temple due to the abundance of monkeys that inhabit the grounds.

The Bagmati River has been polluted for a hundred years less than the Rhine, is much shorter, and is in the control of only two countries. If the Nepalese government were to concentrate their efforts on what occurs in the Kathmandu Valley that the Bagmati flows through, a great deal could be done in a short amount of time to restore the river closer to its original state of cultural and spiritual significance. A cleaner Bagmati river and Khatmandu Valley would also create a stronger economy by increasing tourism and keeping tourists in the Valley for longer periods of time. The communities in the Valley are already trying to move forward, they just need the government to join in.

बागमतीलाई पहिलाकै सांस्कृतिक र आध्यात्मिक महत्वको स्थलमा परिवर्तित गर्न सकिन्छ । सफा बागमती र काठमाडौँ उपत्यकाले अझ बढी पर्यटक निम्त्याउँदै र तिनीहरुलाई उपत्यकामा अझ बढी समय बिताउन प्रेरित गर्दै नेपालको आर्थन्यवस्थालाई पनि मजबुत पार्न महत्त पुऱ्याउन सक्छ । उपत्यकाका समुदायहरु अगाडी बढ्न तयार झन तिनीहरुलाई मात्र सरकारको साथ चाहिएको छ ।

Nepalese residents paste pictures of Naag (the serpent god) over their doorways with cow dung and offer foods to the god to protect their home from lightning, fire, snakes and scorpions

A Hindu woman inside the Golden Temple in Patan wears a red bindi on her forehead symbolizing true love and the site of her third eye where a higher level of spirituality or self realization can occur.

BAGMATI RIVER ARTS PROJECT TIMELINE

February 14, 2014

"Biological Regionalism: Alberto Rey" exhibition opens at Burchfield-Penney Art Center, Buffalo, New York

April 14, 2014

approached by David Johnson at Biological Regionalism exhibition to consider project about Bagmati River in Nepal.

May 1, 2014

met with Tullis and David Johnson at Burchfield-Penney Art Center to discuss project. We decided we need to know if there is interest in the project in Kathmandu.

May 6, 2014

proposal and images from exhibition sent to Sunil Shrestha, an architect in Kathmandu.

May 7, 2014

Sunil is interested in project and Sharad (Anil) Parajuli, coordinator and founder member of Himalayan Healthcare Inc.(an international non-profit, non-governmental organization, founded in 1992) is interested in meeting with us when he travels to US. Meeting is set for September 15th in Buffalo. Since there is initial interest, we proceed with plans.

August 27, 2014

began research on galleries, art organizations, conservation groups, art schools and artists in Kathmandu.

September 2014

researched and studied several government reports, journal publications and newspaper articles about the Bagmati River.

September 5, 2014

contacted by Satya Karki at Sherpa Flies to help them distribute their products in US.

sent proposal about project to Chancellor Mr. Kiran Manandhar, Nepal Academy of Fine Arts.

sent proposal about project to Sangeeta Thapa, Director of Siddhartha Art Gallery, most respected contemporary art gallery in Kathmandu.

sent proposal about project to Friends of the Bagmati.

sent proposal about project to Kathmandu Contemporary Art Centre Residency Program, London, UK.

sent proposal about project to Sujan Chitrakar, head of Kathmandu University's, Centre for Art and Design.

September 8, 2014

Sangeeta Thapa responds that she is interested in exhibiting the work from the finished project.

September 9, 2014

contacted Chancellor Mr. Kiran Manandhar, Nepal Academy of Fine Arts, again.

September 10, 2014

Sangeeta requests participation in the Kathmandu International Arts Festival.

September 14, 2014

proposal is accepted and am awarded a residency at the Kathmandu Contemporary Art Centre.

September 2014

researched and studied more journal articles on the complicated effects of climate change in the Kathmandu Valley and Nepal.

September 18, 2014

submitted application for a Guggenheim Fellowship to work on the project.

September 22, 2014

sent proposal and inquiry about Arts Envoy Program to Camille Benton, Curator, Art in Embassies Program, US Department of State, Washington, D.C..

September 23, 2014

contacted Bronx Museum about smArt Power program, international cultural arts program, and find out it no longer exists.

September 23, 2014

received response from Shannon Dorsey, Bureau of Educational and Cultural Affairs at the U.S. Department of State, and more information on Arts Envoy and American Arts Incubator/Zero1 programs.

September 27, 2014

received response of interest in the project from Sujan Chitrakar, head of Kathmandu University's, Centre for Art and Design.

September 29, 2014

sent proposal about project to Zero 1 and get back response that Nepal is not one of the countries they are serving at this point.

October 10, 2014

proposal about project is sent to artists recommended by Sangeeta Thapa whose work deals with the Bagmati River.

October 29, 2014

worked with Erin Cooper at Hatchfund, the arts fund-raising site goes live as a way to finance project.

November 3, 2014

received email from Tom Gordon, from my hometown in Fredonia, New York, who is willing to accompany me to Kathmandu to assist me while I'm there and sets up a meeting with his brother-in-law, Mike Rechlin. Mike is an expert on Nepal and is Dean of Future Generations Graduate School and past Chair of the Biology Department at Principia College, Elsah, IL.

November 2014

Canon 7D body and wide angle lens are purchased for videos and photography.

November 18, 2014

sent proposal about project and inquiry about Arts Envoy Program to Deputy Chief of Mission John L. Carwile at the US Embassy in Kathmandu.

November 24, 2014

received response from Marisa Polnerow from Cultural Affairs Department at the US Embassy in Kathmandu that there are some staff changes occurring and that the issue will not addressed until the summer.

December 9, 2014

through recommendation of Mike Rechlin, sent proposal of project to Rajendra Suwal, Deputy Director at WWF Nepal, who in return sent it to Shikha Khetan of the Green Generation. The Generation Green (TGG) is an ambitious five-year campaign (2014-2018) of WWF Nepal that seeks to strengthen the engagement of Nepal's youth in conservation and promote smart choices for the environment.

December 19, 2014

grant application submitted to Robert Rauschenberg Foundation, New York, NY to fund the project.

February 10, 2015

sent sponsorship application to Qatar Airways to fund airfare.

February 2015

Canon zoom lens purchased for videos and photography.

February 11, 2015

Rauschenberg Climate Change Grant is declined.

February 16, 2015

submitted application to Creative Capital, New York, NY.

April 7, 2015

Guggenheim Fellowship application declined.

April 25, 2015

7.8 Earthquake hits Kathmandu at 1:40pm.

April 25, 2015

sent email to Sangeeta to check if she is okay.

May 3, 2015

received email from Sangeeta, that the project remains as scheduled but the residency will occur at another site.

June 1, 2015

Creative Capital Project proposal is declined.

September 2015

applied for National Endowment for Humanities Summer Stipend.

project residency is delayed from November 2015 to March 2016 with exhibition in November 2016 due to affects of earthquake on the city.

applied for Living Legacy Project: Artist Support Grant, Burchfield Penney Art Center, NY.

October 2015

sent sponsorship request to 5 airlines.

sent sponsorship request to Osprey Packs, Inc.

applied for sabbatical for fall of 2016.

Jason Dilworth, graphic design professor and conservationist from Visual Arts and New Media Department at the State University of New York at Fredonia joins project.

contacted Splash.org, an international organization promoting clean water in underdeveloped countries.

November 2015

applied for a Carnegie Fellowship.

December 2015

airline tickets purchased on Qatar Airlines and reservations made at Shakya House.

contacted Susannah Fisher, climate expert/senior researcher from International Institute for Environment and Development, London, UK.

got immunization shots for Typhoid Fever and Hepatitis A and B.

December 2015

received funding from Living Legacy Project: Artist Support Grant, Burchfield Penney Art Center, Buffalo, NY.

Sujan Chitrakar, Head of Center for Art and Design commits to project and we make arrangements to meet with his graphic design class to discuss project and look at student work.

January 2016

Hepatitis B booster shot taken.

David Gillette, environmental studies professor from University of North Carolina, Bibhuti Jha, the professor at KU and other environmental experts interested in assisting in the project.

February 2016

purchased www.bagmatiriverartsproject.com and www. bagmatiriverartproject.com domains .

Rajendra Duwal, Deputy Director at World Wildlife Fund Nepal, and Shikha Khetan, Director of WWF's Generation Green Program, are interested in working on the project. We began to work on art assignments for their 16–26 year old participants.

created drawings for t-shirt and sticker design.

project supporters contacted for t-shirt sizes and t-shirts are ordered.

Canon 100mm macro IS lens purchased for videos and photography.

started to pack camera, art supplies, flies and research on snow trout and macroinvertebrates in the river.

February 2016

Dr. Mike Jabot, science and education expert from State University of New York at Fredonia, provides water testing and mapping assistance.

Nick Gunner, founder and owner of Orbitist (mapping program) and New Media Manager for SUNY Fredonia, and interns joined project and began working on maps for project.

Osprey Packs, Cortez, Colorado interested in being a partner in project but will need to wait until next funding cycle in October of 2016 for commitment.

received and studied the recent finished Bagmati River Expedition 2015 report sent by Dr. Mike Jabot. Report has much more comprehensive water test results at 33 sites and information pollution, avian and macroinvertebrates populations, flooding and sanitation patterns. cancel water test kits and contact Carol Milner in Cambodia. Carol was one of the expedition leaders. We requested GPS coordinates for the test sites and to contact info on other expedition leaders in Kathmandu.

March 11, 2016

arrived in Philadelphia and had dinner Mike Jakubowski and his friend, Mike. Stayed overnight at Embassy Suites Philadelphia Airport.

March 12, 2016

in morning, we flew to Doha, Qatar (13 hours) and after a short layover, we continued on to Kathmandu (4.5 hours).

March 13, 2016

arrived in Kathmandu and figure out visa procedure at airport before taking taxi (Ganesh, driver) to Shakya House in Patan. Unpacked and had dinner at Dhokiama Cafe. Got lost on way home in total darkness because of lack of electricity. Found way back to hotel using GAIA GPS app. began our daily blog entries for our time in Nepal (http://www.bagmatiriverartproject.com/kathmandu-residency-march-2016/).

March 14, 2016

had breakfast at hotel and then walked to Patan Dunbar Square and the Golden Temple. Then went to Kathmandu Contemporary Art Center (KCAC) where we met Sangeeta Thapa, director of Siddhartha Gallery, Raleev Sethi, chairman of the Asian Foundation, Pujan Gandharba and Amrit Gandhari, musicians, Suresh Man Lakhe, Patan Museum Director, and Sujan Chitrakar, head of Center for Art and Design at Kathmandu University. We recorded the musicians playing a traditional war song. Got lost again that evening on way back to the hotel. We had dinner at Dhokiama Cafe again since it was the only restaurant still open and it was also close to the hotel.

March 15, 2016

attended "Capacity Building and Design Development for Making Markets Work for the Conflict Affected Nepal", a global craft conference at Yalamaya Kendra in Patan. In the evening, presented my lecture with Bill McAlister, former director of the Institute of Contemporary Art in London. We had dinner at Dhokiama Cafe again because it was located next to lecture venue. At the lecture, met Dr. David Gillette, an aquatic biologist from University of North Carolina who was on Fulbright in Nepal. We corresponded before trip and he grew up in Fredonia, New York.

March 16, 2016

went to Boudhanath, a UNESCO heritage Site and sacred Buddhist temple, and continued on to Shivapuri Nagarjun National Park to find the Sundarijal sample site on the Bagmati River Expedition report. Bagmati River Expedition report was an important part of our exhibition, book and project. Created two drawings and shot photos and video of the sample site. We all drank filtered water from the river and got lost again that evening looking for the Roadhouse Restaurant. We ended up again at the Dhokiama Café.

March 17, 2016

met with Dr. Deep Shah, water quality specialist and part of the Bagmati River Expedition team, Shristi Vaidya, from the Nepal River Conservation Trust and Jeff Davids, water specialist and president of H2Otech, at Kar.Ma Coffee in Patan. We discussed the project and got their perspective of issues related to the Bagmati River. Dined that evening at Thai Ghar in Patan.

March 18, 2016

met Swodesh Shakya, our hotel owner's brother and our guide for the day, and Ganesh, our taxi driver from the airport. We documented two other sample sites from the Bagmati River Expedition; Gokarneswor neighborhood and Guheshwori Temple/Pashupatinath Temple, two of the most sacred Hindu temples in Nepal. We also went to another sacred Buddhist Temple, Swayambhunath Temple (Monkey Temple). We ended the evening at Thai Ghar, which had become one of our favorite local restaurants.

March 19, 2016

in the morning, we were surprised to find an article about our March 15 lecture in the Kathmandu Post, "Building an Art Movement" by Mark Harris (http://kathmandupost.ekantipur.com/news/2016-03-19/building-an-art-movement.html). After breakfast, we went back to Guheshwori Temple and a community painting event of professional artists depicting their aspirations for the Bagmati River. The event is sponsored by and located by the High Powered Committee for Integrated Development of the Bagmati Civilization which is also the location of the city's only partially-working waste water treatment plant. We documented 16 artists and their paintings. We also went to our last Bagmati River Expedition sample site in Chovar where we shot photographs, videos and create some drawings. We had dinner with David Gillette and his father-in-law and brother-in-law at the Roadhouse Café in Patan

March 20, 2016

Prince Edward came to Patan Museum but we left the museum before he arrived. We filmed and recorded Pujan Gandharba and Amrit Gandhari and the song we commissioned for the documentary about the Bagmati River. We headed back to High Powered Committee for Integrated Development of the Bagmati Civilization to photograph all the high school artwork entries for their "Dream of the Bagmati River". The twelve winners were reproduced in a calendar. Later on, met with Sangeeta Thapa and updated her about the project.

March 21, 2016

videotaped my interview with water quality specialist, Dr. Deep Narayan Shah, and climate change specialist, Dr. Ram Devi Tachamo Shah, at the KCAC. Was interviewed by Albaya Joshi from onlinehabar.com and Smriti Basnet from the Nepali Times. We had dinner with Dr. Deep Shah and Dr. Ram Shah at Casa Pagoda in Patan Dunbar Square.

March 22, 2016

it was the Hindu holiday, Happy Holi, so we could not arrange any interviews. No one wanted to meet for fear of being pelted with color pigments and water balloons. Young hotel owner, Saajan Shakya, and his brother, Swodesh, took us to a crowded joyous rave-style celebration at an old hotel that afternoon. We met Dr. David Gillette at Kilroy's in Thamel for dinner.

March 23, 2016

met with the Director of the Patan Museum, Suresh Man Lakhe, to photograph a watercolor of the Bagmati River created in 1800s and photo from 1900. He also gives us a tour of Patan Museum grounds and a buildings. There was no electricity during the day, so we could not see the collection in the museum. We interviewed and videotaped Sujan Chitrakar, the Director of the School of Art and Design at Kathmandu University and Dr. Bandana Pradhan, Professor at Institute of Medicine at Tribhuvan University. We had dinner with Dr. Bibhuti Jha, an aquatic biologist from KU, who has done extensive research on the snow trout in the headwaters of the Bagmati River. He could not get us permission to document the snow trout in Shivapuri Nagarjun National Park.

March 24, 2016

visited Erina Tamraker's and Asha Dangol's studios in Patan. We also met Sangeeta Thapa at her gallery and discussed details of the exhibition. Afterwards, we took a tour of Kathmandu Durbar Square and saw several important cultural structures that were damaged by the recent earthquake. We dined with Sangeeta at Fire & Ice Restaurant in Thamel (Kathmandu).

March 25, 2016

We met Sangeeta and then interviewed Leela Mani Poudel, former Minister of Cultural Affairs, who was instrumental in working with organizations to create the weekly Bagmati River clean ups. Afterwards we went to Barbar Mahal Revisited in Kathmandu to meet with William Holton, Cultural Affairs Officer from the US Embassy. Later, we interviewed Sangeeta's 89 year-old father, Mr. Himalaya Shumsher J.B. Rana , who held various government positions in the past. We flew out of Kathmandu that evening on Qatar Airlines.

March 26, 2016

we arrived in Philadelphia and then flew to Buffalo, New York where we were picked up by Dr. Mike Jabot.

March 27, 2016

"The chronicler of rivers comes to Nepal" article appeared in onlinehabar (http://english.onlinekhabar.com/2016/03/27/373506).

April 2016

accumulated more research material and started organizing text for publication.

April 2016

project t-shirts were mailed to sponsors.

April/May/June 2016

wrote essays for publication.

May 2016

received Hep B booster shots

May 2016

scanned each page of sketchbook, finished artwork, and organized photo files.

June 2016

worked with Sujan Chitrakar, and Ms. Ujala Shrestha and their students at Kathmandu University to design public health brochures, posters and artwork for the project.

June/July/August 2016

organized the text, photographs and artwork into chapters and designed the project publication.

June 2016

met with Nick Gunner, president and founder of Orbitist (www.orbitist.com), and Christine Doolittle to discuss mapping and microsites options for the project website.

June 2016

Alex Maiola edited sound files from interviews and music for the project documentary.

June 2016

airline tickets were purchased.

August 2016

sent files to printer.

Osprey Packs contacted again about their interest in sponsoring the project.

project documentary "BAGMATI" was finished.

received Hepatitis A booster shot.

August 2016

updated David Johnson and curators from the Burchfield Penney Art Center, Buffalo, New York, Scott Propeack and Tullis Johnson.

August/September/ October 2016

worked on artwork, graphs and website.

September 2016

lectured about the project at the Association of Great Lakes Outdoor Writers Annual Conference in Mayville, New York.

October

lectured about the project at the International Trout Congress in Bozeman, Montana.

November 2016

artwork exhibited at Benjaman Art Gallery, Buffalo, NY. A percentage of sales was donated to the Bagmati River Art Project.

November 11 - 25, 2016

traveled to Kathmandu to present exhibition, documentary and website. Distributed book and public health brochures and posters to communities in the Kathmandu Valley.

arranged for return of artwork from the exhibition at the Siddhartha Gallery in Kathmandu to the United States.

December 2016

continued working with Scott Propeack and Tullis Johnson from the Burchfield Penney Art Center in Buffalo to organize the project's touring exhibition.

Alberto draws in Patan Durbar Square as a child looks on.

10:00 Am - 10:55 Am - Patan Durban Square, Patan, Nepal - March 23, 2016

Jason takes a selfie in a taxi somewhere in Kathmandu.

Project Leaders

Alberto Rey was born in Havana, Cuba. He received political asylum through Mexico and has resided in the United States for fifty years. He is an artist, a Distinguished Professor at SUNY Fredonia, an Orvis endorsed fly fishing guide, and the founder/director of Children in the Stream, a youth fly fishing program. His artwork has been in approximately two hundred exhibitions and is in the permanent collections of twenty museums in the United States and Europe.

www.albertorey.com

Jason Dilworth has a BFA in Visual Communication from Weber State University, Ogden Utah and a MFA in Graphic Design from Virginia Commonwealth, Richmond, Virginia. He teaches Graphic Design and Typography at SUNY Fredonia in the department of Visual Arts and New Media. His work reflects a love of geology, history, ecology, mythology, mysticism, conceptual, performance, and folk arts.

www.jasondilworth.com

Alberto tries to soothe his cough by drinking lemon tea and honey at Chez Caroline before our meeting with William Holton from the U.S. Embassy in Kathmandu.

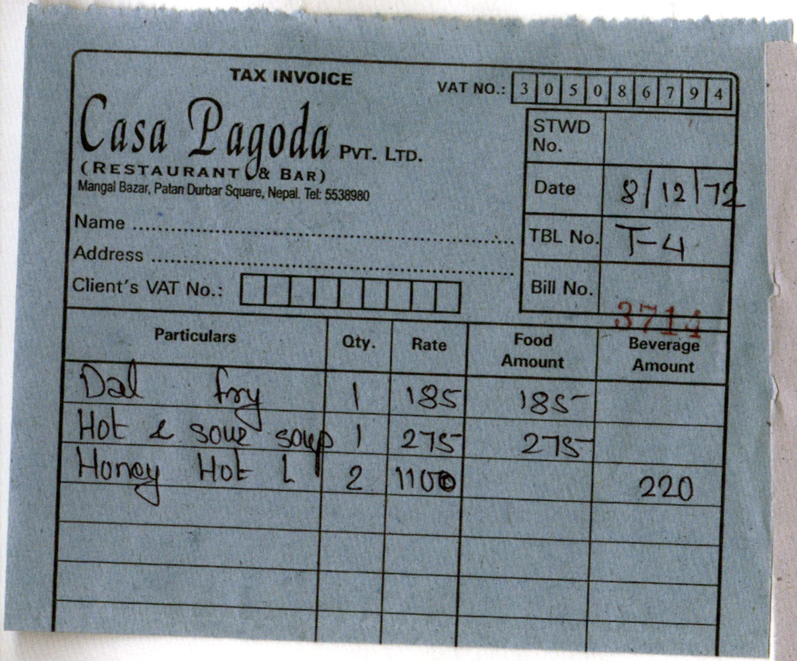

TAX INVOICE

VAT NO.: 3 0 5 0 8 6 7 9 4

Casa Pagoda PVT. LTD.
(R E S T A U R A N T & B A R)
Mangal Bazar, Patan Durbar Square, Nepal. Tel: 5538980

Name ....

Address ....

Client's VAT No.: ☐ ☐ ☐ ☐ ☐ ☐ ☐ ☐

STWD No.

Date 8/12/72

TBL No. T-4

Bill No. 3714

Particulars	Qty.	Rate	Food Amount	Beverage Amount
Dal fry	1	185	185	
Hot & sour soup	1	275	275	
Honey Hot L	2	1100		220

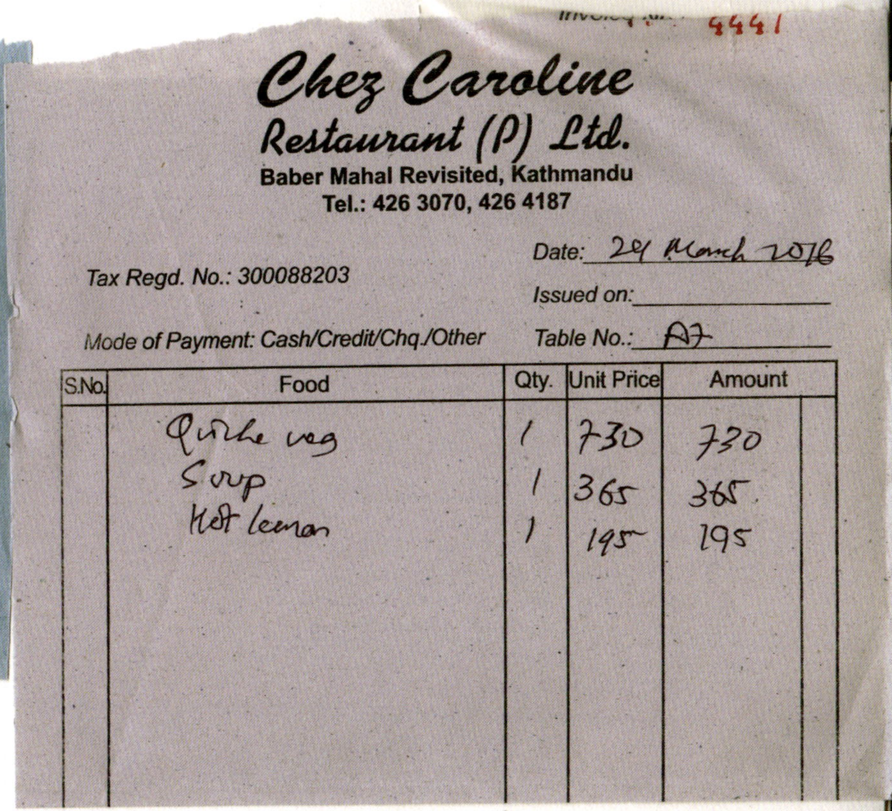

Chez Caroline
Restaurant (P) Ltd.
Baber Mahal Revisited, Kathmandu
Tel.: 426 3070, 426 4187

Invoice 4441

Tax Regd. No.: 300088203

Date: 21 March 2016

Issued on: _____

Mode of Payment: Cash/Credit/Chq./Other

Table No.: A7

S.No.	Food	Qty.	Unit Price	Amount	
	Quiche veg	1	730	730	
	Soup	1	365	365	
	Hot lemon	1	195	195	

Restaurant receipts from Casa Pagoda near the Patan Museum and Chez Caroline, an upscale restaurant, next to the Siddhartha Gallery.

During the day, the dogs in the Kathmandu Valley rest in preparation for their evening-long barking sessions that turn to howling as day breaks. By early morning, they are sleeping again.

References

Chaubey, V.K. and Forbes, W. *The Holy Bagmati River.* Varanasi, India: Pilgrims Publishing, 2015. Print.

Hannigan, Tim. *Nepal.* Hong Kong: Apa Publications Ltd, 2014. Print.

Knowledge Base-the United Nations World Water Development Report 4. Vol. 2. Paris: United Nations Educational, Scientific and Cultural Organization, 2012. Print.

Pradhan, Bandana. *Water Quality Classification Model in the Hindu Kush-Himalayan Region: The Bagmati River in Kathmandu Valley, Nepal.* International Centre for Integrated Mountain Development, 2005. PDF File

Bagmati River Expedition 2015, Nepal River Conservation Trust and Biosphere Association, 2015. PDF File.

Kathmandu Valley Environmental Outlook. International Centre for Integrated Mountain Development, 2007. PDF File.

Bagmati Action Plan (2009-2014). High Powered Committee for Integrated Development of the Bagmati Civilization and National Trust for Nature Conservation, 2009. PDF File.

Hoirala, Shishir. Improving Water Security in Bagmati River Basin, Nepal. Network of Asian River Basin Organizations. PDF File.

Bagmati River Basin Improvement Project. Asian Development Bank. 2014. PDF File.

Jha, P. and Shrestha, K. (2013). *Climate Change and Urban Water Supply: Adaptive Capacity of Local Government in Kathmandu City, Nepal.* Journal of Forest and Livelihood, Volume 11. PDf File.

Jha, P. (2012). *Climate change: impact, adaption and vulnerability in water supply in Kathmandu valley.* WIT Transactions on Ecology and the Environment, Volume 155. PDF File.

Environment assessment of Nepal: emerging issues and challenges. Asian Development Bank and International Centre for Integrated Mountain Development, 2006. PDF File.

Bagmati River Coming Back To Its Original Form. Food and Agriculture Organization of the United Nations, 4 Sept. 2014. PDF File.

Ravat- Francoise, Emmanuelle. *Marketing Safe Water in Nepal: Community perceptions of chlorination and other water-purification methods.* Universtat St. Gallen 2014. PDF File.

Summary Environmental Impact Assessment – Melamchi Water Supply Project in the Kingdom of Nepal. Asian Development Bank, 2000. PDF File.

Green, H., Saik-Choon, P. and Richards, A. *Wastewater Treatment in Kathmandu.* Massachusetts Institute of Technology, 2003. PDF File.

Dahal, Achyut, "Khanal, Mausam and Ale Megh. "Bagmati River Festival: Conservation of Degrading River." 2011 Georgia Water Resources Conference April, University of Georgia, Athens, GA. PDF File.

Paudel, Arjun. *Environmental management of the Bagmati River Basin.* Environmental Impact Assessment -United Nations University 2009. PDF File.

Sivec, Ignac. *Notes on Himalyan Stoneflies from the Collection of Zoologische Staatssammlung Munchen.* Spixiana 5.2: 181-186. 1982. PDF File

Shrestha, Jiwan. *Coldwater Fish and Fisheries in Nepal.* Fish and Fisheries at Higher Altitudes: Asia -Food and Agricultural Organization of the United Nations, 1999. PDF File.

Rai, A.K., Pradhan, B.R. , Basnet, S.R. and Sawr, D.B. *Present status of snow trout in Nepal.* Cold Water Fisheries in the Trans-Himalayan Countries - Food and Agricultural Organization of the United Nations, 2002. PDF File.

Regmi, Megha. *Feasible low cost sustainable options to maintain river quality: Case of Kathmandu Valley Rivers.* International Riversymposium 2006. PDF File.

Green, Hillary. *The Effects of Carpet Dye on the Bagmati River.* M.I.T., 2003. PDF File.

Platman, Lauren. *From Holy to Holistic: Working Towards Integrated management of the Bagmati River Corridor*. SIT Graduate Institute 2014. PDF File.

Fisher, Susannah. *Nepal: Measuring resilience to climate change from the community up. International Institute for Environment and Development*, 7 Feb 2014. Web.

Kathmandu Declaration: Recommendations for financing communities most vulnerable by climate change. International Institute for Environment and Development, 7 Feb 2014. Web.

Gautam, Subodh. *How a great river is vanishing*. Climate Change Media Partners, 22 Jun 2015. Web.

Kathmandu highly vulnerable to climate change impacts, Climate Himalaya, 23 Jul 2011. Web.

The dead rivers of Kathmandu, Climate Himalaya, 1 Jun 2011. Web.

Adhikari, Debesh. *Kathmandu Vulnerable Climate*. NewsSpotlight Nepal, 5 Aug 2011. Web.

Regmi, Megha. *Feasible low cost sustainable options to maintain river quality: Case of Kathmandu Valley Rivers*. International Riversymposium 2006. PDF File.

Green, Hillary. *The Effects of Carpet Dye on the Bagmati River*. M.I.T., 2003. PDf File.

Harmon, Lin. *Saving Nepal and the Planet, One Lawsuit at a Time*. Advocate Magazine Fall 2011. Web.

"Over 150 aftershocks felt since Great Quake." The Kathmandu Post 9 May 2015: News. Web.

"Clean Bagmati Campaign: 60,000 people to join mega drive in 100th week." *The Kathmandu Post* 22 Mar 2015: Capital. Web.

"17 metric ton solid waste extracted from Bagmati river." The Kathmandu Post 6 Feb 2016: Capital. Web.

"Bagmati Mahotsav begins to mark 150th week of Clean Bagmati Campaign." *The Kathmandu Post* 27 Mar 2016: Capital. Web.

"Art exhibition on Bagmati." *The Kathmandu Post* 23 Mar 2016: Entertainment. Web.

"Clean Bagmati Campaign enters 138th week." *The Kathmandu Post* 3 Jan 2016: News. Web.

"Bagmati clean-up in 150th week." *The Himalayan Times* 3 May 2016: Kathmandu. Web.

Pradhan, Tika R. "More and more people suffering for COPD, says docs." *The Himalayan Times* 20 Mar 2016: Nepal. Web.

Thapa, Gautrav and Adhikari, Anuj. "Kathmandu: The third most polluted city in the world." *The Kathmandu Post* 19 Mar 2016: Capital. Web.

"Not enough roads for Valley vehicles: Traffic Police." *The Kathmandu Post* 9 Jan 2016: Capital. Web.

Thapa, Gautrav. "Half of Melamchi waters 'to be used' for Bagmati regeneration." *The Kathmandu Post* 30 Aug 2015: Capital. Web.

Shahi, Pragati. "All out efforts to revive lost glory of Bagmati." *The Kathmandu Post* 4 Sept. 2011: Development. Web.

"Treatment plant to run on overdrive-Melanchi water supply project." *The Kathmandu Post* 10 Aug 2015: Capital. Web.

Thapa, Gaurav. "No water at the end of Melamchi tunnel." *The Kathmandu Post* 21 Mar 2016: Capital. Web.

"Water getting scarce for Valley folk." *The Kathmandu Post* 3 May 2016: News. Web.

Mayton, Joseph. "Can the Kathmandu Valley be Saved? " *The Ecologist* 26 Sep 2012: News. Web.

Mishra, Dinesh."Bagmati River: From holy river to flowing filth." Rediff News 12 July 2012. Web.

Misra, Tanvi. "How Urban Planning Failed Kathmandu." *The Atlantic: CityLab* 26 Apr 2016. Web.

Four rivers One World-Bagmati, Educational and Cultural Affairs Bureau, U.S. Department of State, 2008. Web.

"Leakage adds to valley drinking water woes." *NGO Forum for urban Water and Sanitation* 20 Dec 2010. Web.

Adhikari , Nanda Bikram. *Detection of Leak Holes in Underground Drinking Water Pipelines using Acoustic and Proximity Sensing Systems.* Research Journal of Engineering Sciences 2014 . PDF File.

Freeman, C., Khanal, N., Satti, W., Upreti, A., Webster, G. *Melamchi Water Supply Project.* Fuqua School of Business, Duke University 2014. PDF File.

Kathmandu Population 2016. *World Population.com.* Web.

Upadhyaya, Bhim. "Suicide Bagmati Civilisation?!." *World Water Day: Challenges of Water for Present and Future Generation in the Kathmandu Valley* 10 Jan 2011. Web.

Lorch, Donatella. "You Think Your City Is Full Of Trash? Ha!" *NPR* 23 Mar 2015. Web

Karin. "Garbage: A Big Problem of Kathmandu." Everest Uncensored 2010. Web.

" Nepal Population Estimates." Flowfinder.org 1 May 2015. Web.

Udamale, P.,Ishodaira, H., Thapa, B.J., and Shakya,, N.M. The Status of Domestic Water Demand: Supply Deficit in the Kathmandu Valley, Nepal. Water Journal - Multidisciplinary Digital Publishing Institute 2016. PDF File.

"Quake, dry spell worsen Valley's water woes." *The Kathmandu Post* 12 Mar 2016: News. Web.

"Tap water." *The Kathmandu Post* 4 May 2016: Editorial. Web.

"Managing Nepal's Urban Transition." *The World Bank* 1 Apr 2013: News. Web.

Thapa, Rajesh Bahadur and Murayama, Yuji. *Examining Spatiotemporal Urbanization Patterns in Kathmandu Valley, Nepal: Remote Sensing and Spatial Metrics Approaches.* Multidisciplinary Digital Publishing Institute 2009. PDF File.

Panr, Pradip Raj, and Dongol, Devdra. *Kathmandu Valley Profile.* East West Center 2009. PDF File.

Oliver, Rachel. "All About: Developing cities and pollution." *CNN* 11 Mar 2008: Asia. Web.

Kattel, Dambaru Ballab. "Water Borne Disease a Major Health Problem in Nepal." *Ohmy News* 6 Dec 2007: International Globe Watch. Web .

Corcoran, E., Nellemann, C., Baker,E., Bos, R.,Osborn,D., and Savelli, H. SICK WATER? THE CENTRAL ROLE OF WASTEWATER MANAGEMENT IN SUSTAINABLE DEVELOPMENT. United Nations Environment Programme 2010. PDF File.

Grung, Anadeeta and Sharma, Sudodh. "Water Quality And Response Of Macro-Invertebrates To Damming In Bagmati River At Sundarijal, Kathmandu, Nepal." National River Summit, Dhulikhel, Nepal 2014. ResearchGate. Web.

Salike, Inu Pradhan. *Kathmandu Valley, Nepal - Climate Change Vulnerability Assessment.* United Nations Human Settlements Programme (UN-Habitat) 2015. PDF File.

Chitraker, Anjil. "Gokarna". *ECS Nepal* 21 Jul 2010: Heritage Tale. Web.

"Nepal Energy Situation. " *Energypedia*: South Asia: Nepal. Nepal. Web.

Grad, Paul. "Nepal: Moving Mountains in Melamchi." *Waterworld* Vol 31 Issue 1: Waste and Water International. Web.

"The lake that was once Kathmandu." *Nepali Times* 6 Aug 2010 – 12 Aug 2010: Life Times. Web.

Integrated Development and Management of Water Resources: A Case of Infrawati River Basin, Nepal. International Water Management Institute 2001. PDF File.

Pandey, V.P., Shrestha, S., and Kazama, F. *Groundwater in the Kathmandu Valley: Development dynamics, consequences and prospects for sustainable management.* European Water 37: 3-14 2012. PDF File

Pandey, V.P., Chapagain, S.K., and Kazama, F. *Evaluation of groundwater environment of Kathmandu Valley.* Environmental Earth Sciences 60:1329–1342 2010. PDF File.

Sethi, Makriti. "Competition for Hydropower in the Himalayan Region: The Complex Regional Scenario." *Science Technology and Security* Forum. Web.

Nepal Tourism Statistics 2014. Ministry of Culture, Tourism & Civil Aviation 2015. PDF File.

Shrestha, A.B., Wake, C.P., Mayewski, P.A., Dibb, J.E. *Maximum Temperature Trends in the Himalaya and Its Vicinity: An Analysis Based on Temperature Records from Nepal for the Period 1971–94*. American Meteorological Society 1999. PDF File.

"Nepal Unemployment Rate 1991-2016." *Trading Economics* Jul 2016. Web.

Dixirm, Ajayu. *Inter-Sectoral Water Allocation: A Case Study in Upper Bagmati Basin*. International Water Management Institute. PDF File.

Suwal, Sahisna. "Water in Crisis – Nepal." *The Water Project*. Web

"Water Quality and Pollution Control in the Rhine River Basin. " *AquaPedia Case Study Data* 20 May 2014. Web.

Bernstein, Richard. "Rhine has fish again, but it's not as it was." *New York Times* 20 Apr 2006: Europe. Web.

Patan Square, Patan, Nepal - 12:40 pm - March 17, 2016

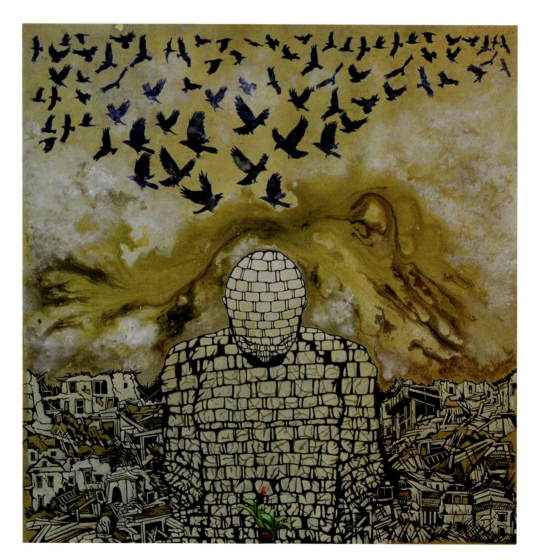

Asha Dangol *Aftermath*

Asha Dangol *New Beginning II*